Adytum

Mary Cools

One Printers Way
Altona, MB R0G 0B0
Canada

www.friesenpress.com

Copyright © 2025 by Mary Cools
First Edition — 2025

All rights reserved.

No part of this publication may be reproduced in any form, or by any means, electronic or mechanical, including photocopying, recording, or any information browsing, storage, or retrieval system, without permission in writing from FriesenPress.

ISBN
978-1-03-832505-1 (Hardcover)
978-1-03832-504-4 (Paperback)
978-1-03832-506-8

BIOGRAPHY & AUTOBIOGRAPHY, PERSONAL MEMOIRS

Distributed to the trade by The Ingram Book Company

"The spirit of love, once freed from our mortal bodies, will blow where it will, even when few will hear its coming and going."[1]

Henri Nouwen

---

[1] Henri J. M. Nouwen, *Life of the Beloved* (N.Y., New York: The Crossroad Publishing Company, 1992), 125.

Table of Contents

The Revival	1
The Guilt	15
The Survivor	25
A State of Mind	35
Liberation	43
One Unit	51
Survival Guide	61
The Leavening	67
At Odds	89
God Has a Name	97
A Fine Day	103
Emotional Deadness	109
The Farm . . .	125
Felt in the Heart	133
Epilogue	137

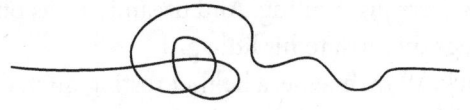

The Revival

I remember being nine-years-old and I could hear grasshoppers chewing. It was *that* quiet on the banks of the Welland Canal. I could smell sawdust because it was Saturday, and my father was with me after his half day in the lumberyard. I can still see the world being grand with the bright colours of fall. Still feel the prickly roughness of crushed hay on my back as we lay on the steep canal bank surrounded by uncut hay. I knew the world was grand because my daddy was there, and we had collected a full bag of acorns for the squirrels living near our home. This was our job since my brothers were away doing manly things. They were much older than me.

The sky was blue to the ends of the earth and fluffy white clouds painted pictures for our perusal. Daddy had twisted my long, blond hair around one of his strong hands so that we wouldn't need to brush the grass from it later. My hair was his pride. I wore thick glasses so he felt it would be my redeeming factor come marriageable age. He brushed my hair often and I his, at least what was left of his hair. He often told people that I had pulled most of his hair out of his head while brushing. But I knew the real reason for his shiny scalp peeking from beneath his careful comb-over.

"Daddy, what's that one look like?" His wrinkled, tanned, forty-something face smiled his gape-toothed grin from his nest in the long grass next to me. The crisp smell of fall apples drifted on the breeze around us as he looked up thoughtfully. We had all the time in the world since we were just waiting. And dreaming was one of the most important things on earth to his little girl.

"I think a rock. With, maybe, a helmet resting on it. Or a head with a helmet. Yes. A head with a helmet."

"A helmet?" I asked. I was just not seeing it. Really, he had no imagination! But I knew why.

"Yeah."

"Daddy, it's turtles!"

"Yes! Turtles! That's nice. Not a helmet. And . . . no guns," he decided.

"When do you think a ship will come by?" I was getting tired of waiting and the acorns we had collected for the squirrels needed to be put into the baskets put out for them in our yard. It was very important to my nine-year-old heart that they not go hungry during winter. I had learned about hunger.

"Soon. You need to learn to wait better."

"I am waiting just fine," I whined. "But the squirrels are probably hungry at home."

"Wait. Sometimes we have to wait. So do the squirrels. Sometimes we have no choice. I want to see a ship from Europe, from home!"

I did not want another lesson on how hard it was to wait. I'd had that lesson a number of times, at length. So I waited some more.

"You want to see a ship from Belgium?"

"Yup."

"How about from Holland? France? Germany?" I named the countries that I knew bordered on Belgium. "That would be almost like a ship from home!" I had been studying geography in school and wanted him to know that I had learned about Europe. My being smart was important to him. It would be another redeeming factor.

"Not Germany! From anywhere. But not from there. They shouldn't come here."

I did not question my father about why the German ships shouldn't come here. I knew better than to open that can of worms; I knew that, even at nine years old! I saw that his eyes had already turned away from the clouds and his thoughts had turned inward.

That was always a bad sign. I could sense that something was about to go horribly wrong. His sky was growing dark with his own private shadows. It was like watching children playing on a beach and seeing a storm building on the horizon. Onlookers cringed, knowing that the tempest would overtake the happy children in minutes. The finest day would become a ruin.

"Let's collect some more acorns! We didn't look under that oak tree over there." I pointed. He did not look, so I took his hand, as my mother had taught me, and stood up, still pointing.

He released my hair as I stood. Then wiped his face with shaky hands made rough by work with lumber. He stood up too. "Let's get those nuts then." His smile looked more like a grimace but my infantile plan had worked. He was back. Sort of.

I watched my father as we gathered more nuts. A few crickets were singing accompaniment to our work. I wanted to sing along but I knew that my off-key voice was a disappointment to my father. He was musical. I was not, not in any way. His sisters' daughters could sing. I could not hold a tune. But I knew that he was proud of my ability to listen and understand things. He told people that I was smart. That made me feel proud. He could be a hard man to please.

As I scurried around the tree, I watched his short, tanned arms reach for nuts. His smile opened into a more sincere grin when I squealed at another full bag. But I was thinking about him. I was trying my hardest to understand the shadows in his eyes on such a glorious day, while he was with me, collecting nuts for squirrels.

I focused on his smile. He had a few missing teeth. He always said the war had stolen his teeth, left them rotting from lack of proper care for five years. I always wished that I had seen the teeth my mother described to me as whiter than white and straight as those seen on toothpaste commercials. I thought he was handsome. Thinning hair and missing teeth were of no significance to me where my father was concerned. He was the air I breathed.

"Here comes a boat!" I shrieked. I was so very excited! We always shouted welcomes to the sailors, and they always answered us!

* * *

"Shit!" my father swore. "Get behind me!" He grabbed my arm roughly and I felt each of his fingers bruise me. And he was shaking with rage.

I cringed in fear, not daring to peek from behind him. Something menacing was most certainly drifting toward us and I could not tell what it was. "Wh . . . what's wrong?" I whispered.

"Shut up, Mary! It's the Japanese! Goddamned allies of the Germans." He held me behind him and piercingly spat out, "Fucking bastards! You won't make us run; we are not afraid of you! I'll take your damned boat and shove it up your asses!"

The freighter was almost halfway past us, at this point. My father stood tall, his entire five-feet, five-inch frame rigid. He raised his right arm as though he was going to salute *Heil Hitler* but turned his hand up and proudly displayed his middle finger to the sailors watching with their eyes wide with disbelief.

Twenty years meant nothing in my father's world. Young as I was, I realized that fact then, at that very moment in time. I learned that hate never dies.

The ship passed as some sailors, standing below their red dotted flag, "saluted" my father in return and in the same way. He never let go of my arm, just remained, finger raised, until the ship was a half mile away. Then he dragged me home as though he had forgotten his vice-grip on my arm.

As I stumbled along, my only thought was, "They shouldn't have come here."

We reached our doorstep; my father released me only when my mother gently asked him to. She patted my head and rubbed my bruised arm softly.

"What happened?" she breathed into my father's red face. "You are scaring Mary!"

"Goddamned Jap ships, that's what!" my father shouted. And my mother shooed me back outside.

I sat on the stoop, crying because we'd left all of the nuts on the canal bank and I pictured my squirrels hungry and cold. I pictured them the way my father had described—hunger and cold.

At the time, I thought they were the tears of any disappointed nine-year-old.

However, much later, I realized that I was not crying for any childish reasons. I cried because of my father's darkness; and because I loved him. And he could be terrifying.

I remember being nine years old.

* * *

Now, years, no, decades later, I sit at my desk with a picture of my parents watching me. They cannot speak to me anymore. I cannot touch them, and they can no longer touch me. I miss them every day. The bright sunshine, the same rays that shone on my father and me by the canal that last day we ever went there together, shine outside my window. I feel like I am waiting for the fall, the change, a change so that my memories of my parents can emerge more vividly for me. My parents loved the fall, the colours, and their children—but not in that order. They taught me to think before I speak; that is what I am doing right now. I am at my desk, ignoring God's outdoor brilliance, just thinking. I am thinking about them and why I cannot cope with their loss. "I am a big girl now," I tell myself, "an adult. I should be able to move on." But that is absolutely not the case. I cannot do this—live without them. Something must be wrong with me.

I let out a heavy sigh and closed my eyes, willing myself back to that last time I collected acorns with my father. I had relived it, more than once. This was not the first time I'd hashed out that episode in my life. But it was the first time my eyes shot open with an idea.

Recently, I had learned a new word: adytum. It means a place filled with awe and reverence for being alive. Usually, this awe reaches forth from places we revere like a church, temple, synagogue, or the like. It touches us while we feel near to God. I say "usually" because for me, my adytum existed as an obscure place inside of me—a holy shrine deep, deep within me. I thought of it as my soul.

Well, I remembered more now. When I was nine, I cried because my adytum cracked. It broke within me, leaving me, to this day, with emptiness and loneliness. I remember feeling like the Christmas movies had ended and the Christmas tree had once again been packed away while I was left staring blankly toward the empty corner where the magic had stood.

I now understood for the first time in a very long while what my journey was to be. I needed to rekindle my adytum. Where to start was the question. So I talked it out.

* * *

I want to remain true to my past. My past is a part of me and as both my mother and father have become my past, their history is mine too. Still, I have trouble seeing the past clearly, with bold images of them dying always clouding my eyes. I long to hear their voices again, guiding me, but the sounds of their last words block out any whispers I might hear.

It is not always easy. The last words of a dying loved one will always anchor to a morsel of thought in the listening, living minds bidding them goodbye—however, my mother had words only for my father.

My father said one word, only for me.

Do I feel the weight of words too profoundly? Is that what shields me from reviving my soul? Or is it the burden of what was not said that hinders me so that I feel I cannot journey onward? Perhaps it has something to do with the fact that I am very much like my father and maybe I like it that way. He had never truly brought back his soul from the concentration camp where he grew up, in Germany.

During my childhood, I believed that my brothers had become aloof. I barely saw them while they were busy living their lives away from home. I thought brothers were the strong ones; the ones who needed no familial support. Like their father.

Wrong.

I realized that my father's image of male strength was wrong during my mother's last heartbeats. I recognized that my brothers suffered, just as fully as I did, as we witnessed her feeble heartbeat stop.

They were not aloof.

I looked up into my oldest brother's eyes. His tears blinded him and he reached out to his two brothers, who bracketed him. They both had white-knuckled grips on the railing of the hospital bed. They looked away but I saw that their hearts were breaking. There was only a relentless emptiness in the room as nothing was said between us.

My three brothers touched one another on that far side of the bed as I held my father, alone, on the other side. I always felt destined to be the one left out. Too young. Then, too girly. Always, too emotional. But now, we all shared this grief. We were finally together, as my mother had always wanted us to be. It only took her death to show us what we were too stubborn to learn from her. Another crack, almost audible, released the last shreds of adytum that I possessed. (This is not where my downward spiral had begun. It is a long story. But this is what I came up with during my thoughtful afternoon.)

"If only she had taught us to speak with one another," I thought sadly. Instead, I had stood and watched them suffer, as they had watched me. Would my burden seem less than it does now if we could have comforted one another? Would I still be here now, sitting here thinking, alone? It is years after my parents' deaths and I have not moved on.

I am stuck without a soul.

* * *

"Do you know where the washrooms are?" my mother asked my father. It was her last sentence before we lost her. He did not speak. He could not speak.

I answered. I told her that I would love and care for him in her absence, so she could close her eyes in final peace.

I would care for my father through his incontinence and worse. And I would care for him for my family, who could not be as near.

He lived for four years without her.

"S'okay," he told me as he lay dying. Dialysis had been stopped before the cancer could give him pain. His body was being poisoned from within. He knew that his journey was over. I saw that much in his eyes. He faced his death with a bravery which rendered me speechless.

I knew he wanted me to tell everyone that he understood it was his time and that he was accepting it. He existed back in a happier time already; it was a time when both he and my mother had been younger and whenever things did not go right, it was still okay. That is what I told everyone who asked what his last words were. In truth, he was talking out loud with my mother as he fell into a peaceful sleep from which he never awoke.

Some weeks after my father passed, typed pages blurred before me. I blinked. I turned my head away from the papers I was staring at, essays my grade-ten students had attempted for the first time. Mesmerizing comments on the literature we had read, *The Book Thief*, each trying to convince me of something they had discovered about the novel. I just could not comment on their efforts right now. For the first time, the thought that it could be time to retire burned behind my weary eyes. I felt like real life lay elsewhere for me.

And there lay the key.

I had to find my life again. I had to regain my equilibrium and take the reins of becoming the matron of my family. How? This was the question I could not answer.

My gaze drifted out the window of my portable, situated outside the high school where I felt that I had taught literature for too long. I could see the canal from that window and loved that I had been assigned this particular room. I noticed for the first time that the sun had snuck a bit too low over the water for me to still be at work. I would have to get the caretaker to unlock the main building again, for me to grab my purse and the rest of the work I wanted to do over the weekend.

I really needed to stop searching for a way to cope with my life while on the job. I was getting nowhere in both departments. For now, I simply needed to get home.

Adytum

***

"Hello! I'm home," I called as I entered the front door.

"Hi! I thought you'd never get here! You're late." My husband, Rudy, knew where I had been and what had happened. It happened so often that I did not need to explain. "Did you get any marking done?"

"Not really . . . I was away again. Far, far away this time."

"I know." He paused and kissed me for reassurance. "I miss them too."

"I lost track of time," I explained needlessly.

"Sure you did. You must love that job!" he joked.

I could not hide my grimace. "We need to talk."

"Can we eat first? I made supper. Roast chicken and salad!"

"Thank God. I am starved!"

We filled our plates and made our way out onto the deck outside our kitchen door. Fall was spectacular this year and we did not want to miss any more of it than we had to.

"How was your day?" I asked. It was how we began every single one of our evening conversations.

"Same bull, different day!" he answered. "We sent some huge lunch orders out to the Best Western today. They ordered almost everything on the menu. Some conference or something." He never batted an eye over the amount of work he did. As a chef, he had the necessary calm demeanor to survive the industry.

"Good to keep busy, eh?" I quipped.

We laughed gently as the peaceful fall evening wrapped our cares in its comfort and the singing of crickets lulled me toward the past, again. We ate in silence for a bit, just enjoying the quiet which our jobs stole from us during the day. But I could not remain content this evening.

"I think it's time for me to retire," I said bluntly. We had had this discussion a few times before but this time I meant for it to be final.

"You do qualify for it . . . but you've always changed your mind before."

"This time I mean it. I just can't cope with work, this emptiness I feel, and the responsibility I feel toward my parents' legacy. Why can't I move on with my life? I think I need to concentrate on living life. I feel like I'm coming apart at the seams."

"Hey, take a breath." He hugged me from his seat beside me at the table. "I'm sure we can figure something out. If you need to retire, then do it. How does just after Christmas sound? Just after this semester? Maybe then you can finish sorting your parents' things and you'll feel some closure?"

"Maybe." I was not convinced that getting rid of more of my parents' things would be the answer but I felt comforted that the decision lay entirely in my own hands. I would give my notice in the coming week. There was relief in that thought alone. I would no longer feel I was giving my students only half of the attention they deserved.

Soon after we ate, my husband, an early-morning chef, went to sleep in preparation for another grueling shift. That left me free to escape to the past without feeling I had abandoned him. I smiled to myself as I watched our near neighbours organizing a campfire. And, with my anxiety a bit lighter, I felt I could now enjoy the smoky smells of an autumn evening and dream my Friday night away.

* * *

Surely, the key to happiness lay somewhere within our cores, in the person we were born to be. In my case, I felt it lay in who I was brought up to be. In either instance, our happiness should be found somewhere inside of us where we can still be full of awe, translucent, and quick to spark a belly laugh; somewhere I myself had not visited for some time. Not since the day I saw a Japanese ship and my father's post-traumatic stress disorder stole my soul away. I did not want to be trapped in my father's somberness anymore. But I could feel bits of myself slipping toward that darkness every day. Somehow, I had to remember his joy! I believed that the key I had found was in his joy. There hid my reverence for the privilege of being alive! But had he experienced enough joy in his life?

Adytum

***

Thoughts about my father's joy led me to our family vacations.

My father never planned anything in his life. Our fishing trips were a haphazard collection of excitement and unlooked-for events. He decided we were going, my mother planned a few meals, and we were off! Three teenagers, me, and our dog, Bob, all piled into the two back seats of our station wagon. My parents in the front seat, endlessly trying to find the right roads to travel. "A few meals," for my mother, meant pots full of homemade food and enough ingredients to feed an army stacked between her children and the dog in the back seats. Between my parents rested at least two suitcases of clothes. That car was packed with no room to move. Each of us children held boxes of something and complained the whole way about cramps and stiffness where we could not move under our burdens. My father was all smiles as he yelled, "Fish beware! We are on our way!"

Another aspect of our adventure was that our car was never new or serviced. My father drove every car he had ever owned into the ground and this station wagon was pretty low to the ground as we drove the four hours to a cottage we had never seen. Three and a half hours of driving and we reached a dirt road leading into the bush. This was apparently the "driveway" to our cottage. The narrow laneway we could see disappearing into the forest had huge pieces of granite jutting from the ground and through the surface of the packed dirt. We rounded a bend too fast, and one of the back tires exploded as it hit a granite speed bump.

Bob flew out of the seat furthest back in the wagon and landed on my mother's lap in the front seat. His feet had not touched my brothers in the back seat and I now sat, open-mouthed and alone, in the seat at the very back. My father hit the brakes and yelled, "S'okay! We can walk the rest of the way and check if they have a spare tire!"

Stone-faced, my mother asked, "We have no spare tire?"

My father just grinned. He was in his element, happy and joking all the way into camp. My mother waited for her spare tire in the front seat of the wagon. She was "not amused." She was an advocate of regular service on the car. Car upkeep was an ongoing battle of wills in our home!

***

"S'okay!" I said aloud. I was grinning from ear to ear.

My family needed to hear that story again, for sure!

The scent of woodsmoke drifted toward me on the warm autumn breeze. I could hear the children next door busy making s'mores. I caught myself imagining the warm and cozy atmosphere of an evening on a remote campsite. It was a world that seemed a million miles away from the everyday.

I closed my eyes and allowed the tranquil scents and sounds to lull me back into my thoughts of a past I could not leave behind. I still felt as though I could not move on. Maybe retirement would bring a chance for peace. The semester could not be over soon enough for me.

***

It was fairly late on Sunday evening when I finished filling in comments for my students' essays. I was proud that some of them had actually absorbed my constant nattering about how to formulate a convincing argument. Others had been in a world of their own and needed work. I knew how that was; it was getting more and more difficult for me to concentrate on their progress rather than on my own agenda. Retirement was quickly becoming the logical choice for my next step in life. Perhaps then, I could concentrate long enough to make sense of the fact that I could not get past my loss.

I had to find a way to put closure upon my parents' lives. Perhaps by sharing their memories somehow? I felt that I needed to search for a way to do that.

I glanced at the clock: 8:30 pm. It had begun to rain earlier so the roofed deck outside seemed cold and damp, too much like the feeling of loneliness I was battling. I made tea and closed the bedroom door on my sleeping husband. His shift began in the middle of the night and I could use this time to think. Our lives worked out perfectly although I sometimes wished he could be awake longer to talk things out with me. He was such a rock for me that I missed his logical perspective toward my dilemma.

As always, when left alone with my thoughts, I rushed to find answers to questions I had not even thought of yet. I did not switch on a light, the gathering darkness, inside and out, suited my purpose. The steam rose from my cup to curl and surround a family portrait on the wall. All of my family seemed to hold a collective breath in that photo moment. They were all waiting for me to figure this out. Finally, I realized that I was not the only one who suffered. My brothers needed the path that I sought as much as I did.

"S'okay." I swear I heard my father's approval—instead of the silence I expected.

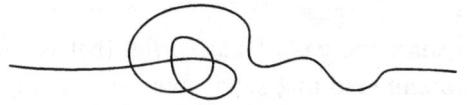

The Guilt

I fell back into the lazy-boy chair. It was done. I had retired from teaching. I already missed my students and it had only been three weeks since semester two had started. But I was done. I glanced around my cluttered home office; my eyes rested first on the boxes of teachers' paperwork and paraphernalia, leaning precariously against one wall. Those boxes could wait some more. As my eyes traveled the cozy room, the winter sun leaking through the window highlighted the two wooden dressers left over from my parents' home. Those two sets of drawers and an antique clock were pretty much all that I had inherited from my mom and dad. Still, I had not, in the four years since my father's death, been able to deal with the task they presented.

I shook my head. I wanted to leave those treasure chests closed. I feared what the contents would put me through. But I felt I should sort through my heritage in order to find any missed mementos I might want as keepsakes. My husband had told me, more than once, that he thought I would find closure in the task. I was not so sure. I felt like closing my parents' chapters in life would require much, much more from me. What form *much more* would take, I could not even guess. I closed my eyes to block out the enormity of my dilemma. Immediately, visions of our family history, snippets of the past flew to the forefront of my mind. I could not escape this. It felt like something needed to break out from deep within me. Maybe if I could share the past somehow—

My eyes flew open! Again.

I needed to share the past! Hadn't I felt that way before? I had! When I had remembered that story about our family's fishing trips, I'd felt like I needed to share that with everyone. To remind them of—our history! The idea somehow seemed right. But what in the world did I have to share that was at all noteworthy? My eyes shot to the two chests of drawers, my vision pulled by the beam of sunlight that seemed to shine from heaven upon them. Those last remnants of my parents' lives had stood dormant, waiting, for four years.

From out of nowhere, the thought that I had missed something crucial skittered through my mind. I suddenly felt like whatever my parents had intended by leaving me these two seemingly benign pieces of furniture had been lost on me. This thought somehow seemed to beckon to me from within the darkness of the drawers. Suspicion that my parents had made some sort of last gift for me niggled at my soul.

Maybe I could throw together some sort of family album or something to distribute to all of my family members? I knew there were plenty of photos in the drawers. I stood and wandered, hesitantly, over to the chests; was I ready to face the pain that beckoned to me?

For a second, as I looked at the closed drawers, I felt very alone. I had been worrying and uncomfortable about my parents' deaths for so long. Was I so friendly with that feeling of unease that I could put off opening up their lives again? I stood gazing down at the dressers. I stood in front of the only physical pieces of my parents' lives that were left to me. I reached out and opened the first of the sliding vaults protecting me from my heartache and looked inside.

* * *

I have always believed that mothers and fathers paint their children's lives with stories. My parents were artists. I listened to their stories often and just as often, I witnessed their hearts drifting away from me during the narratives. Their faces would become overcast while the stories I listened to concentrated on pictures of Belgium, Europe, a war, a voyage, and family members left behind. Yet my parents still wielded the brush and created their lives for me. Both my mother's and my father's memories created for me a sense of what made them who they were. The world Mom and Dad described for me was coloured by some dark secrets. I learned from a young age why they held their secrets inside to only rarely spill out during the most awful conversations.

Of all that my parents had seen and experienced, I could only learn what they chose to depict. They told me only what I, with my determined presence in their lives, begged to hear. This blotting of memories is what has made me who I am today. My mother liberally peppered me with stories on an almost daily basis. But my father kept history inside his head, locked away. I am more like my father which makes this journey most difficult for me.

* * *

I found myself standing in that ice-tinted shaft of sunlight, staring at a plain manila envelope. Not a very big one but it was thick. It was just lying there beneath some photos of boys in snowsuits, boys riding bicycles, my mother holding a baby girl, my parents standing in front of a new car; and now, here was this envelope that I had never seen before.

It had my name on it.

My name was printed, unevenly, in my father's large block letters.

It did not say, "Mary."

He had used my full name.

So, this envelope had been very important to my father.

Beneath my name he had written one more line:

FOR MARY COLETTE COOLS
MY MEMORIES AND EXPERIENCES

The breath caught in my throat when I reached out to stroke the words.

My father had had something to say to me for years. I had asked him for his memories many, many years ago. I had thought he wasn't strong enough to relive his nightmares.

And then, I believe I heard my mother whisper, "Ohhh-hhho! She found it!"

I removed a bundle of handwritten notes from that envelope. I held the penciled papers to my heart for just a moment. This felt like the hug I had needed for far too long. Then I looked down at the words my mother had written on the first page.

That was when I felt my heart stop beating and my soul bled out.

> We cannot be with you when you read this story. It is pain to us. And, our boys, show them this last work of ours when they can't remember us.

I held my father's life—it was neatly written in my mother's hand. I held their pain in my hand.

* * *

When I was seventeen years old, I watched my father's face twist into a horror with aversion so intense that it changed his features. I had caused this transformation. I had requested the impossible from him. Sometimes teenagers say things that cause parents to cringe but this was unforgivable. I knew better than to push my father too far but I had still done it without a second thought.

The conversation had begun innocently enough.

"I know that with Peter attending Guelph University, we can't afford another tuition for me, Dad. I am okay going to Niagara

College. I can study Chemical Engineering Technology for now and still get a good job."

"I know that would work, Mary. But I feel so badly you cannot study English Literature like you really want to."

"I can study Literature as a mature student when I have saved some money. Chem. Eng. pays well."

"I wanted to send you to school, just like Peter. You are both so smart."

"John and Albert are smart too and they're doing just fine with college educations. I'll be okay. I'll write someday. You'll see." He smiled at me and stroked my hair. "You can write down your memories and experiences in Belgium and I can turn it all into a great memoir!"

Without thinking, I had turned a tender moment into bitterness that sparked in the air between us. His face twisted grotesquely with an internal struggle I could not even begin to fathom. I felt panic rise as he swallowed loudly. Undiagnosed PTSD does not need any form of assistance to ruin lives.

"You don't need to write about the war," I added breathlessly.

Without a word, he vomited into the bushes beside his lawn chair.

I had done this.

His eyes filled with tears. I felt like I had turned on him.

I *had* turned on him.

I knew that conversations with my father should never go back in time.

What had I been thinking?

He heaved again.

What had I done? I ran inside for something, anything, to calm him. Finished retching, he accepted the clean washcloth I had run for.

Then he shook his head, miserably.

I wanted nothing more than to take back the words I had just spoken. But words, once spoken, cannot be taken back, ever.

To this day, the idea that I had only been a thoughtless seventeen-years-old at that time still does not excuse me. I bear the guilt.

***

And now, I held all of that pain in my hands. He had revisited his nightmares—for me—because I had thoughtlessly asked him to. I had brought him a world of hurt and he had been strong—for me. I had never loved him more than at that moment.

I saw nothing but the tears which blinded me.

I heard my husband come home from a shopping trip and wiped at my eyes before he came in.

"Ah! I see you started to tackle the job, finally! It will be good for you. How is it going?"

"Fine." I cleared my throat and tried to hide my misery from him.

"Fine?" he asked. "You don't sound fine at all. What's wrong?"

I sniffed. "I know what I need to do to get through this depression over my parents. I need to write. My dad wrote me his memoirs and I cannot just read them. They need to be shared. Our pain needs to be released. I know he suffered to write this." I held out the memoir notes.

His arms came around me. "He loved you so much!" he whispered. "That could be the best decision you've made since retiring. If nothing else, it will be therapeutic."

"Yeah . . . but it's sad that my dad's pain is the only way for me to find closure."

He tightened his arms around me. "It will be comforting for everyone to read about that remarkable man. Come into the kitchen; let's eat this takeout I got. Chinese will make you feel like you can do this." He smiled into my eyes as I realized that writing was the only way out for me.

***

"My Memories and Experiences." Other than the title page, the memoir was written in my mother's delicate handwriting.

"Mommy's writing is really something. I can't write like that." I heard my father's pride in my mother's penmanship once again. It was as though he had breathed it in my ear just now. The imagined sound of his voice gave me the strength I needed to read the penciled words. I began to read as my mind raced in and out of times.

> Unlucky day for me... they caught me! They chained me to my bike. That is how I was forced to travel with them.
> Chained.

"Daddy... Daddy... Daddy... Da... ddy... did you see it? Daddy... *are* you listening?" I pulled on his sleeve.

"Hmm? Did you say something, Mary? I was just..."

"You said to just look ahead and I wouldn't fall over. I did it. I rode my bike all the way from there!"

"I am watching, Mary. I'm watching. Do it again. You can do it. Go on."

> "We're watching you. Pigs! Do it again if you know what's good for you. Sweaty pigs! That's what we like to see." The unexpected blow hurt. Did they break my ribs? I have to survive. How long will the running go on? I think we are running toward our deaths.

"There! I did it!" His eyes had glazed over again. "Daddy?"

"That's great, sweetie. Stop before you get all sweaty; it's hot out here."

My father's silence was something I recognized. It happened too often and my mother had told me he needed his privacy then. So I said nothing more. I did not want to provoke his rage or his sadness. God only knew which way it would go with him and his silences.

My father's silences were bits of him that I could absorb, feel. Even as a child, I sensed where he went, why he went, why I was not taken there; his anger and forlornness enveloped me at these moments when I watched him slip back in time. His unintentional teachings made me a miniature empath. I was not closer to him than my brothers—I was more emotionally malleable, and therefore less liable to question his silent ability to convey to me his many shades of black. I just sat with him and imagined his burden becoming lighter when his arm snuck around me.

* * *

"It's called *Papillon* Dad. You'll like it. It's got a lot of action and a guy goes to prison when he didn't do the crime. He tries and tries to escape; he's even put into solitary. *And* it's on Devil's Island." My oldest brother, John, loved movies.

"I don't like to go to the movies," Dad told him, his eyes remote. His vision had turned inward the instant he took in the movie synopsis.

Standing a little on my own, I turned toward their conversation. But, eerily, it had turned to silence. The future of the day lay in that void during which John and I waited.

> Chained together like murderers. We hadn't done anything wrong! My parents were there to see me marched onto a train like a criminal—I saw them for five minutes as I tripped along. My mother was screaming, "He's only a boy . . ." That's how long it took to load us like evil cargo.

"I'd rather work on this old radio, John," Dad continued vaguely. "Let's fix it together. I just got my diploma you know. Now I can fix all sorts of appliances for people. You can help me; come on."

"Can we feed the birds first? I want to see if the chicks are ready to come out of the nests. When will you sell them?" John wanted to know.

"Don't know. Not ready. Yes. Let's feed the chicks first."

John did not seem to notice the choppiness in our father's words. Or that his eyes had lost all their light.

"You thirsty, Dad?" I intervened. "I'll get the mason jar. Mom made fresh cold coffee." I tried desperately to take my father's mind off his eighteen-year-old self. I knew that he could not forget that he, too, had been punished for something he did not do.

> Still chained and being humiliatingly dragged to the centre of the city, in the heat of midday, was bad. It is nothing! I'm thirsty. The dryness is so overwhelming I can taste it like a flavour; thirst is everything! In this unfamiliar, empty building all afternoon with just the heat and smell of overheated bodies, I'm wondering if this is where we will all die. I could die here.

"Dad... you want the cold coffee?"
"I guess so. Bring it down with you. I'll have some while John and I work in the basement."

> The Red Cross! They have brought food and drink! Suddenly this prison feels less like death. I have no complaints about the provisions—our country has not forgotten us. Our country will save us!

* * *

My memories, unbidden, mixed with the memoir notes. I could actually see where some of my father's comments had originated. And reading his words brought clarity to certain links my brothers and I could make in the blink of an eye. We could be brought together as family in a split-hair moment by our history. Dad's mason jar of cold coffee lived on like a bittersweet smile that would not leave us. Memories of childhood never vanish from our inner eye; just as my father's memory of being eighteen-years young, and in chains, never died for him. But that memory had been a secret. Until now.

Are some of us enslaved by our memories?
I can still see Dad at his shirtless work.
I still recall Mom in her hot kitchen and loving it.

Are these memories a comforting escape? Or rather, is it torment or ecstasy to know these sights as though I lived them yesterday? These things I remember were their self-expression, the knowledge of which sometimes drowns my attempts at clarity as I recall lives more important than my own, at length . . .

My toil with words is their legacy—an eloquence they could not accomplish on their own. The work is grueling and makes me feel like it may not turn into anything of worth. But just knowing that any result will bring integrity to our family and to our history is enough to make me go on.

Sometimes, I go to the canal bank and just sit where my father and I used to sit. I went there after I had asked him to write his memories down. I remember the temperatures of water and air had mingled then to create a mist so thick that I could have buried my sorrow in it. But I could never lose the memory of the agony on his face; I still carry it. Foggy days are haunting for me; they carry a world of guilt.

The Survivor

I am standing on the dikes beside the canal, near my home. The air smells clear and clean as I take it in. It feels like ice passing through my nostrils to accost my lungs with frigid air. I stomp my feet to warm them with friction but my toes do not respond well. At least, since I feel the jarring of them inside my boots, I know that they are all still alive and well. I am not frozen yet, so I just keep walking. All I hear is the crunching of frozen snow beneath my feet between intermittent howling gusts of wind. There is no powder snow here; only miniscule bits of ice exist, frozen together to form a barrier to the ground beneath and to my wandering boots above. It is not just cold. It is bitter cold. It hurts to taste the wind as it barrels down the corridor made by the banks on either side of the canal. It is like a racecourse for the air here in February. There are no leaves on the trees now to soften the gale that blows into my face but I find a strange comfort in the frostiness surrounding me. The icy atmosphere here is invigorating and life giving, especially to someone as melancholy as me. I know the bareness of the dikes, slanting away from me on either side, will be replaced by living bounty in the spring. But for now, the stark trees serve their purpose for me. I am here to seek clear thoughts. I walked away from my warm desk an hour ago desiring this solitude which God provides every winter.

Remembering is always a battle of sorts for me. My mind resists painful memories, and thoughts themselves become like moths at a light bulb bouncing here and there after battering my mind. So my memory, my history, sometimes defies my efforts to revive those who left me so long ago. And although foggy days at the canal bank are hurtful to me, days like today are a clarifying balm.

I came here today with one purpose: to clear my mind. I need to pick which "moths," which moments, should survive the melee in my mind. As matron of my family, which memories should I choose to bring our family members closure? The dazzling white landscape around me has yet to produce any answers to my questions. I need to decide which thoughts might link my family back together as one. Which memories will draw together the separate, lonely members of my family? We are like broken spokes on a wheel, each spinning out of control on a different lateral course. Our minds never meet.

Now my emotions drift from complete distress toward relief, then back again as I fight to make decisions for my whole family. Is this even possible? I need to get back to my desk. The answer lies somewhere there in a jumble of paperwork I asked my father to produce. He went somewhere he had not wanted to go. He did this for me. There is no escaping this inner battleground of mine; just as there had been no escaping the forces that worked against my father. I will finish this story. I will do this for him.

* * *

I shed the layers of outdoor clothes and my despondency at the door. Then I trudged toward my slippers and to my desk. I needed to get back to work. It was time to revisit the memoir and relive my deepest feelings, which could be difficult for me to share at times. For me there was always pain involved in remembering.

> But—we lost count of how many times we were hit and kicked by our guards. We had arrived on a Saturday and by the next Saturday, twenty-three men had escaped. This infuriated the Gestapo. The experiences of those left behind in their *care* cannot

be put into words ... we paid a price for those who got away.

The barely shrouded darkness surrounding many parts of my father's life had always forced me to stop thinking about the worst details of his story. I feel that was a good thing—a protection against his inescapable gloom. What I managed to avoid dwelling upon probably saved a good portion of my sanity. A world grown too dark can leave scars.

But now, I sit at my desk and force myself to remember *everything*.

When I was young, my mother prevented those scars, and I can never thank her enough for living her life for her children. The stories my mother told soothed my mind at times when empathy for my father became a cumbersome burden. Her memories were a magnet for me; at times, I'm sure, they were so for my brothers as well. But with concrete evidence of those memories so far overseas, I also think that the old stories often became difficult, if not impossible, for "the boys" to picture. My brothers were stark realists ... like their father.

During her narratives, my life became a blank canvas for her to fill with images. I believe my imagination saved me from sheer misery when I had listened to my father for too long.

I searched for meaning in my mother's stories. They were so simple. The art in my mother's history preserved the simplicity of a life she had lost; but it was not lost on me. Her stories took me across the world to Belgium. I traveled there, where I found some of the people involved in her lost life. I spoke with uncles and aunts who had been included in the parties, joyful work, and the loves of her childhood. These people helped me to understand how such a joyful woman could have given up such a life. It was to accompany my father on his journey to find *new* joy, thousands of miles away, in Canada. I saw how she supported him in his hours of need, his head in her lap while his heart bled.

Three prisoners were left dead at the end of tortuous brutality and all were now terrified to be shipped

to Germany. Three days later, we were shipped into the unknown. We knew that maybe we would never see our parents, and all those dear to us, again. We knew that some families followed the buses that took us to the train station in Antwerp. There, from afar, we caught a glimpse of parents, if they were recognizable from the distance. I saw my mom and dad. I was able to wave once. Speaking to them was impossible—it was an extremely sad goodbye. More than four hundred boys and fathers were separated from their families...
WHY?

"S'okay, Daddy. Tomorrow is Father's Day—a day for our children," my mother reminded him. She never left him to brood. She always brought him back to us from the deep sorrow in his soul. Father's Day was always joyful.

* * *

After my mother's untimely death, I began thinking deeply about her. And even though she was no longer with me, I learned to understand her more. At age thirty-one, she carried me to term after three miscarriages, after the birth of three sons prior, and long after her childhood. Yet she lived her childhood again through what she shared from the palette of her life. She knew she had to protect us from becoming too caught up in empathy and sorrow for something we could never have had any control over. She saved me from reliving my father's horror which I was entirely too apt to do. I *lived* and laughed, again and again, inside my mother's stories.

The Runner

"There was a girl named Agnes in my class. Oh, I think we were in grade seven then. She had always been in my class. There were about fifteen of us who went through school together. I could run fast. I was the fastest. Agnes could run fast too but she couldn't stop! And she couldn't turn when she got up to speed. We all knew about Agnes' 'problem,' and we used it to tease the nuns at the girls' school."

"We would all run straight for the nun on recess duty and then turn really fast just before we got to her. We always turned with just enough room for Agnes to turn too. But one day it was icy and we turned a bit too late . . . they both fell, pot over tea kettle, with the nun at the receiving end of the run. The nun had us doing lines for three days. Agnes was never allowed to run on school property again—she was labeled 'dangerous.' She spent a week doing extra sewing during recess. We spent a month trying to make up with her. In the end, we were friends again, but we never stopped teasing her about being 'the runner' in our class."

This story is a part of me. It is a story my mother told when my father was too dark to reach and I was too young to understand him. The last time she told it, ice was rattling on the windows and she was laughing loudly, as she always did. I always felt safe then, when she laughed.

* * *

My father's memories lacked safeness. His moods left him longing for safety, as his stories always left me.

> As we traveled through Belgium, they gathered more prisoners in Tienen and Brussels—up to two thousand men now packed our train. We were all

boys and men gathered against their will to work in *damned* Germany. All had left loved ones. All reacted when the next child was torn from his father's arms and the father taken! We were all taken by our *damned bastard* enemies. After days of traveling, the train arrived in Halberstadt, in the heart of Germany, and 1000 kilometers from home.

If I could re-enter my childhood, I know I would feel the anger my father carefully instilled in my young soul. Now all I can summon is pity for those men and boys, including my father, *and* for the German men forced to carry out such horrendous acts of inhumanity. I know my father would deride me loudly and forcefully mock my pity for anyone German.

I can almost still hear him yelling, "Jesus Christ, Mary! Are you stupid? They're worse than scum!" He would insist on rage and many times my young self would emulate his venom. I would try to hate anyone my father hated. But I was never at war with anyone. I really had trouble seeing the evil in my classmates, even if they were of German descent. My confusion left me broken. My adytum took many blows. I wanted to support my father. I think every child does. I just could not go that far into his darkness. A sense of awe and reverence for the privilege of being alive—was I not supposed to have this just because the world had been at war?

I can still see my mother after my father's harsh words at the dinner table one evening long ago. Her eyes had become hooded as he began his tirade about the Nazi occupation of Europe. She snapped into action as he finished but it was with a shiver, not with a smile. Silently, the dishes were cleared and washed, and everything put away. Silently, she put us to bed. Then, in the silence after bedtime, I heard my father cry and her murmurs of reproach for the pollution of our impressionable minds. It was at times like these that even my mother did not understand his need to have his children hate what he hated. I now understand his vehement hatred and I believe that, in her heart, my mother did as well. She just did not want that hatred as a part of our heritage. I am glad she was there for us. She was the leaven in all of Dad's bread—I know she lightened *my* burden when listening to our father began to filter his PTSD into me.

> In Halberstadt all of us were gathered in a big hall where they lay down the law. Just like *assholes*—they would punish us for three months straight even though we had done no wrong. A white paint mark was put on our backs and on a knee of our pants as some sort of recognition mark. We were forced to work twelve-hour days in an airplane factory. Many days they added hours and it became seventeen to eighteen hours of forced work per day. Food was lousy and scant for three and a half months. During that time, we were bombed by the Allies—that was the worst!

In his memoirs, my father had avoided the episodes of his ordeal which hurt him the most. I now realize that he had told me bits and pieces of his ordeal over the years rather than record them. As I read his notes, I understood that he wanted me to remember and fill in the blanks he was forced to leave. Fear has a long reach. Fear's tendrils could creep through years of trying to forget. I think recording some things too horrible to write in a memoir, would have broken him all over again. The terror had been too much for an eighteen-year-old prisoner of war.

* * *

When I was twenty-three, my father cried for the safety of my unborn children. Halberstadt had stolen his God-given right to feel safe. I was seven months pregnant with his fourth grandson and he came to me shaking with fear for the future of his grandsons.

"Mary, I can't forget! Albert's boys, John's son, your little guy... what if anything like Halberstadt happens again? Even here it isn't safe. It could happen anywhere. It happened to me! I never told anyone ... everything ..."

"What? What happened there? What haven't you been able to tell us?" I begged him while bile rose in my throat like lava. My son kicked violently as I pleaded, "Please, tell me now!"

"I never told Mom. No one. But we have young grandsons now ..."

"What Dad?" I was beginning to panic. "Is this something that can hurt our children?" German doctors had performed unspeakable experiments on some men. Was my father one of them? Was there something sinister awaiting his grandchildren? Had the Nazis intentionally infected him with a disease he could pass on to his family? Or was this fear more of the dark side of PTSD which I had not yet encountered?

Then he broke his long silence.

***

My father had lied by omission in his memoir. When he wrote of Halberstadt, he left out the parts he had told me before my son was born. Just reading the name of that city in his notes made me shudder with renewed anxiety.

The Gestapo did not just *punish* their prisoners for three months as my father had so carefully stated.

The prisoners of war had been kept in a small, empty warehouse in Halberstadt, on Van Diepenbeek Straat. Thousands of men had been crammed in very close quarters. There was only one door leading out of the warehouse. It was no bigger than any normal house door. It was made of steel. The loading bay doors at the opposite side of the warehouse had been sealed to prevent escape.

And a swinging battering ram had been hung from the rafters. It could swing like a pendulum, to and fro, toward the one small door leading out of harm's way. It swung every day for an hour. It swung through the crowd of innocent men who could not always escape its crushing blows. If anyone stopped running, they would be shot dead.

The small door would open for one hour every day. The heavy ram would swing. It either crushed men or pressed them through the small door. Men were brutally damaged. Some with broken limbs, others with broken backs, but all were trampled by the thousands of feet fleeing the ram toward the door and to the relative safety beyond it.

Every day, my father slipped through that door while hundreds of terrified bodies pressed around him. One of his friends, a boy from the village where they both grew up, perished beside my father. His head was crushed between the ram and the steel door jam. His hand slipped from my father's fist as he fell, and my father slipped through the door with his friend's brains splattered in his face and on his body.

My father remembered that blood and bone and brain and shuddered into my arms as he told me of the horror he feared for my unborn son. "These boys cannot go through that," was all he could choke out. "Your little son..."

There was nothing I could say. I hugged my father's shaking shoulders and we both cried. He cried for the safety of his grandsons. I cried for the wellbeing of their grandfather's mind. He was still being tortured, years after Halberstadt.

Both sets of tears were full of terror at atrocities perpetrated in our world. No one knows what sufferings occur behind enemy lines of any kind, anywhere. Even here, where it is "safe."

I remember sobbing a prayer, out loud, for my father's memories to fade and leave him in peace. His eyes did not lie; my father knew that God could not answer that prayer.

"I hope the boys never hear this, Dad."

He shook his head, and I knew this would be the only telling. Until now.

* * *

To break our father's tension, we could always count on our mother to ask a question about our day or give Dad second helpings of his dinner to lighten the mood surrounding him like a shroud. For us, maturing was a slippery slope; my mother took some time to perfect her measurements of lightness. By the time we were old enough to sense the darkness in the atmosphere enveloping our father, our mother had learned enough to keep us a safe distance from it.

Those moments when my father's thoughts drifted to his past, in the midst of the time he spent with us, were his battles with PTSD. During those lapses in his life—during his *separateness*, as I called it, he had learned that there was nothing he could not face. He would set his mind and survive, no matter what. But that aspect of PTSD is frightening when children see it. I saw it after collecting acorns with him on the canal banks.

I learned since then, that he acted the way he did because he was a survivor. He struggled on for his family, for our mother—his beloved wife.

He could not face her death.

I faced her death for him with the stubbornness and skills he had taught me—just long enough for him to survive. But that was all he did after her passing. He survived. He existed.

Then he died too; the history, his story, will always be one of survival.

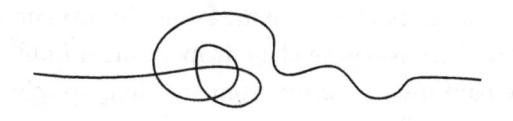

A State of Mind

It seems that my father had promised himself that he would teach his children how to survive. I realized that in my thirty-sixth year. I learned that survival is a state of mind as much as it is a state of being. I was sick; I could feel it in my bones but I did not know what was wrong. My mother told me that my hair looked dull and lifeless, as it never had before, and asked me if I was okay. My father just looked worried when he saw me. My husband prayed. I did look horrible, hollow and drawn, but I thought I was just overworking. That happens to some of us, right? But there was pain.

I was not okay. I had spent the night working. I had finally saved enough money to attend university, to study English literature. It was early winter, almost the end of the semester. I had to complete an essay on Chaucer's "The Knight's Tale," the first tale in his *Canterbury Tales*. It was not due yet but I needed to interpret the tale from its Middle English for a total understanding of the piece; that is what had taken all night, for several nights. I was definitely just overtired.

I stood up to stretch my legs when I finished and that's when I hit the floor. The belly ache which I had been battling, telling myself it was nothing, had blossomed into something sinister in my gut. I writhed in pain. I did not want my children, young teenagers then, to find me on the floor when they got up. I could not shout out and my husband was at work. I could not think.

I gritted my teeth as I had seen my father doing many times in his troubled past. Then using the chair as my crutch, I pulled myself to my feet. The pain prevented me from standing upright so I clawed my way along the walls to my bed. I groaned for help. That is how my children found me. I was rigid on the bed, groaning about death. At least, that is what they told me weeks later.

They called their father for help. I definitely needed help. When my husband came to me, I could not get up on my own.

My parents met us at the Welland hospital. By this time, I was in devastating pain. Worse, no one knew what it was. My family thought I had burst my appendix.

My husband impatiently reminded everyone that the pain was on my left side.

They reassessed.

I lay on that ER stretcher for hours.

My parents and my husband were beside themselves, that much was clear in my mind. The rest became a fog of agony and tests which resulted in more tests.

My husband told me they would figure it out.

My mother cried.

My father told me to think. Think of my children. Think of my husband. Think of them and the rest of my family. Think of Chaucer.

Think. A man who had learned to survive, told me to keep my mind alive and apart from the pain. My family was all around me during the long wait and from their tenacious hope, I formed an unbending state of mind. This was not something that would kill me, I decided. It was just pain, simple and finite.

As it turned out, my pain was something that tried to take my life, just as the Nazis had tried to take my father's life. He knew what would save me if anything could. Survival is a state of mind. This was the only time in my life that I could relate to just how desperately my father had held on to his life. I now had to do the same. He told me so.

The doctors discovered that my intestinal wall had been inflamed for quite some time. They told us that the inflammation was spreading to the outside of my intestines which could now burst. *Acute diverticulitis* the doctors decided. Then before they could operate, the contents of my intestines spilled into my body.

After the rupture, peritonitis grabbed hold of my insides. Infection spread rapidly through me. My situation became, suddenly, desperate. Sepsis was raging through me by the time doctors informed my family that I needed immediate internal repair. And that is when my battle truly began.

The doctors sterilized my abdominal cavity and repaired the fissure in my intestinal wall which had allowed bodily waste to infiltrate throughout my organs. My own bodily fluids had become my enemy. They removed almost a meter of my intestine and created a colostomy which would remove waste from my system while I healed.

My family was told that the peritonitis had spread more rapidly than expected into my blood causing sepsis and thereby, they warned, the inflammation could attack my organs resulting in multiple organ failure and even *death*.

They were advised to pray.

My husband and children prayed.

My mother prayed.

My father chanted to me. I believe I heard him at my bedside.

"Think, Mary. Think. Think. Think. Think."

I know that before I woke from my ordeal, I heard him cry.

I think I heard everyone cry.

My mother told me that I had cried. She had wiped my tears as I lay unconscious, unmoving, and dead to all but my pain.

Weeks later, when I finally opened my eyes, my husband was there. My eyes could not focus. I had no glasses on. But I felt him kissing my hand. When he looked up, a radiant smile lit his face as he stood up to call a nurse. I smiled tightly around the pain caused by the hole the doctors had left in my abdomen. I learned then to hate the word, the very thought of, colostomy. But I also learned to love life and family anew. I had fought a battle and, miraculously, I now knew how my father had survived hell. The hell he lived through had never been allowed into his head. Survival is achieved by keeping an unwavering mindset.

My husband tried to speak to me. His mouth moved silently while his face crumbled and instead, he just sobbed into my sheets. He never let go of my hand.

My son and my daughter came to me there. My daughter placed her head on my shoulder and just lay there for a moment without speaking. With no words I could almost not recognize her, my chatterbox. My son was the quiet one. He held my hand and just looked at me with a sigh in his eyes.

My mother cried, again.

My father's face sagged like a deflated helium balloon when he saw that my eyes were open. The weeks had been a huge trial for him. If I had not survived, I know he would have blamed my death upon his failure to teach me the right survival skills. He was relieved that his mind-over-matter lesson had paid off; that was twice in his lifetime now.

* * *

Survival—a state of mind.

> We were bombed by the Allies—that was the worst! I ran away. I ran through the woods to the top of a hill. I could go no further because the bombs rained all around me. Then I noticed the others around me. I wasn't the only one with hope and terror in their eyes. I hid behind a tree, hoping not to get wounded. One hundred yards around me, in all directions, the bombs just kept falling. They just kept falling—there was no pause, no safety, no hope anymore, just the terror. Just unbelievable fear, again. There are no words to describe a fear like that. It was all consuming; our lives seemed held for a moment by Satan and . . . he laughed at us!
>
> Then there was silence.

That was when we realized we were still alive . . . the laughter, we discovered, was ours.

After the bombs stopped, we were rounded up like cattle. We were forced back to the prison block which had been heavily bombed. I had nothing now but the pants I wore and a pair of shoes.

They put me back to work like this. I had nothing but a thin pair of pants and my worn-out shoes. I worked like this for a month. While most people were given a certificate to get new clothes, I did not get one at the end of the month. Did they run out? I do not know. I know that I remained in only my pants and shoes, working every day, for the next seven months. Those months were from May to December. I remained as I was, burning in the sun or freezing, until finally I was given some clothes. At this time, it had been winter for two months and there was thirty centimeters of snow on the ground. What they gave me was a light jacket to go with my pants so that I could go to work more frequently without dying.

We were bombed by the allies twelve more times but I never lost my clothes again—I was wearing everything I owned. I learned a hard lesson the first time the bombs fell. I learned how to survive. I would see my family again.

***

"Let's get some wine. This is a celebration!" My husband and I had invited my mother and father over for dinner to mark the end of my illness. I had finally undergone the colostomy reversal surgery and had recovered from that enough to say that I felt good.

I felt better than good. "The kids are cooking; maybe we should get something stronger to drink?"

"Or take out?" My husband caught my mood.

Our kids remained serious about their celebratory burgers on the BBQ. I knew that for them it was a tribute dinner. A tribute to survivors!

My mother was organizing the BBQ and my husband was putting out fires. Late summer was quickly turning toward the coolness of autumn.

Slowly, I drifted into a thoughtful mood. I grew quiet. That was when my father joined me and we celebrated life as only those who have been threatened by death can celebrate: with every fibre of our being.

Bees were buzzing between the late blooms in our wildflower garden. Only a stray dragonfly or two remained to drift just above the surface of the pond. They would be gone soon. But my father and I noticed them as individuals. They were each living creatures unequaled by anything else in nature. One blue, one red. One small, one larger and heavy. The huge sugar maple above us clapped its leaves as if in applause of this life we led together. Both of us recognized the minute majesty of the natural world around us; I alone saw it as God's creation. My father remained an atheist, since Halberstadt.

We basked in the stunning beauty of a world which had saved its bounty for us in our time of need. Canada geese flew over on their way to the canal; they would stay for the winter if they could find open water on the Great Lakes surrounding us. Sometimes they left but this year promised to be a spectacular winter. Snow, snow, snow but still mild enough for some black water to remain between banks of ice on the beaches of Lake Ontario. I knew we would drive out to see the lakes in winter and, most stunning, to see Niagara Falls. No ice bridge would join us to the U.S. across the Niagara River this year. The weatherman promised it would not be cold enough. Again, I found God's blessing.

I inhaled to catch the scent of the wildflowers. It was very subtle but it was there for someone who put in the effort to catch it.

Wildflowers rely on colour, not fragrance, to be beautiful. "Can you smell them, Dad?"

"Sure can. I can smell colours!" He laughed. "Can you?"

"I can *now*. I can't say I could have before though." I took his hand. "I guess I just wasn't using all of my senses as I am now."

"Yup. Coming back can do that for you. I hope you never have trouble letting it all in, as I sometimes do, Mary." He raked the garden with his light blue eyes. "I don't want you to be as hard to live with as I am. Stay out of the dark and quiet whenever you can. And when you write, write about something extremely important to you."

That was the best advice my father ever gave me.

*   *   *

Survival.

My parents' deaths were difficult for me to survive as a whole person. I still needed them too much.

I still need them too much.

There is a void.

All that I have left of them—the grandmother clock, the cookbooks, the memoirs—have become barbed nets which catch my thoughts at unexpected moments. At times like these, I must stop what I am doing and think of them. I must relive a piece of my history with them for a moment or two. Only then do I feel like the emptiness inside me is diminishing, as if I am moving toward becoming whole again. I can then sense the person my father taught me to be.

That person needs to reach out to everyone—to share what *family* really means.

These thoughts came from my father. He spoke them to me when he was searching for feelings of safeness. He found shelter within his family and came up with a doctrine: *Families live on as one.*

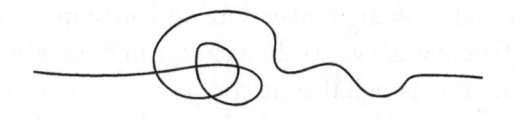

Liberation

As bread envelopes the leaven to make it what it is, my father relied upon my mother for him to be a whole person. He found her, married her, and loved her, in order to capture for himself what he needed to overcome his post-traumatic stress disorder. He had no idea WWII had left him with a disability. He never understood that his bouts of depression were a condition which five years of abuse had caused in him. PTSD is insidious and at that time, an as-yet unexplored frontier.

At times when I experienced his moodiness alongside him, when his shadows were ready to cast a gloominess over anyone and anything around him, he knew his own darkness too. His shades of black were not truly what he wanted for us, and he would cling to my mother's life-giving love to pass *that* on to us instead. His arm would slink lovingly around her shoulders, and instead of a horrible memory escaping from him, he would kiss her cheek and say, "Eh, Madame? Is it good?" She would always smile and laugh. She instinctively knew that simple joy was what he needed from her. She would always tell him she loved him while she hugged him back. My father would be quiet for quite some time after, smiling while he sat basking in her presence. Then, with an almost invisible shake of his head, he could continue on with whatever family activity had once again veered too close to recollection for him.

Although I know my father depended upon my mother for his idea of completeness, when his health began to fail, at age fifty-five, he did not need her strength to endure his hardship. He remained ill for years and there was a very subtle change in their relationship. She had bolstered him enough that he could stand on his own and meet whatever his poor health would challenge him with. He simply held fast to the woman who was the world to him.

My father endured one health issue after another—all of which he blamed on the treatment he had received at the hands of the Nazis. His hatred flared at the unfairness of challenges only God knows why he had faced. We all feared at times that he would leave us forever. He came through each challenge for her and only for her. His illness drew them ever closer, making their love eternally stronger. He lived for the one he had chosen to build his life around and to share his memories with.

Having watched and listened to them live, I am forever thankful for the dark and the light of their collective memories.

> The twelfth day of bombings was the worst. I can't describe it. The liberation troops were coming. The Allies. Shortly after, we saw the first Americans—we were free and we were alive. But we were all very worried about what to expect at home after having gone for eight months without hearing any news from home.

These simple words were all that my parents recorded about the liberation. By our time in history, the world knows what the Allies found in the work camps—skeletal people with fear in their eyes. They found my father, and his friends, with hatred in their hearts. What had been done to them was unthinkable and unbelievable until the Allies actually began to witness the camps for themselves. The world had been oblivious, believing the Nazi propaganda about fair treatment for prisoners of war. The Geneva Convention had not yet been born but those who had created a need for such a document retreated back into Berlin before the Allies could charge them with a crime. Their crimes were never forgiven by my father. "We were free and we were alive;" that was the extent of his joy. He was not yet sure how long he would survive in a world he believed had been forsaken by God.

***

My mother's version of the liberation moved me the most because I wanted to hear the joy—not the uncertainty my father conveyed. I wanted to believe in God's love. My mother's story did not lack uncertainty but it sparked with a life that my father could not relate.

She told me while my father listened—while he tried to capture the joy.

Mom's Deliverance

"It was scary, the liberation. Our town had been occupied by the Nazis since the beginning of the war. People in our town had been beaten—my mother had been beaten by a Nazi soldier who didn't like the way she spoke. She knew no other language than Flemish—she would not apologize for that and . . . he beat her. People in the town had been working with the Nazis—we all knew who they were and avoided them for fear of our lives. Then there was word that the Canadians were coming. Word that the liberation army had finally reached far enough inland to free us. We did not know what to expect. Would there be more fighting? Would this battle finally kill us all? Did the Canadians know we were innocent? Did they know who was not so innocent?"

"The Canadians came, stealthily, in the night. They dragged people into the streets, yelling at them until they were sure who was a friendly and who was a Nazi conspirator. They mouse-holed through our town; small blasts broke through walls and gave access to each new home where the Nazis could be hiding. There were explosions and there was screaming. Our family, mute and trembling, hid in the underground cellar in our yard. We believed that the Canadians would now occupy our town. Would this next occupation be any different than what had happened under the Nazis?"

"Nazi-inspired rumour was that Canada had emptied its prisons looking for new recruits. We feared these soldiers almost as much as the Nazis they came to conquer. We believed the rumours that these new Canadian recruits were murderers and rapists who had enlisted only to buy their freedom; we believed they had no interest in our safety. When they dragged us from the cellar, they towered over us and screamed questions we did not understand. The less we understood, the angrier they seemed to get and the rougher they handled us. I will never forget one brute bending from his great height to whisper something vile into my face. I did not know what he said but I do know that the suggestive gleam in his eyes would have been recognizable to any innocent, young woman like me."

"I was almost eighteen and petite. They were huge, angry men. We thought they were sent into our midst to kill us all. With no hesitation, they had already shot a couple of German prisoners in the back as they tried to run away. One of our neighbours, a conspirator whom we all avoided, was bayoneted as he pulled a small gun from inside his coat; he died in agony as the Canadians walked away to continue their work. No one even looked at the man bleeding out. We were too afraid to look, and the soldiers did not care. That man had tried to kill one of them. Now these brutes probably thought we all had guns hidden in our clothes."

"This realization made me shiver with fear."

"Our family, along with everyone from the rest of the street, huddled in the middle of the cobblestone road surrounded by armed guards. Each one of us feared that with one false move we would be blown away. It was unbearably stressful to not know what would happen next."

"My sister's fear was that of a ten-year-old who had witnessed too much in her short life for this new experience to be anything but devastating. This new threat left her trembling in my arms. She vomited twice before a Canadian medic came to check her out."

"Thankfully, along with the medic came an interpreter. He spoke Dutch but it was close enough to Belgian for us to know what he said."

"And he did not scream."

"Finally, by morning, the German soldiers who had brutalized everyone in our town for five years were rounded up and taken prisoner. Still in fear, we helped the Canadians, who never smiled, to locate the conspirators and the women who had taken Nazi lovers—*how could they?* I guess it was a way to stay alive."

"The interpreter explained the mission of the Canadian soldiers who had terrified us the day before. As those brutes marched their Nazi prisoners out of town, each prisoner with one hand on the shoulder of the man in front of him, the interpreter spoke to all of us calmly and with kindness."

"He told us that those soldiers had been trained to be brutes. They questioned everyone, since they did not know who anyone was. Any one of us might have shot them in the street or as they entered our homes."

"This was war."

"They took no chances and treated everyone like the enemy, as they had been trained to do, while they had searched for the Nazis who had lived in our homes. Caution reigned as they searched for those who had helped the Nazis in their efforts to control Europe."

"Yes. They were brutes."

"But they were angels in disguise."

"They were good men. Not murderers. Not rapists."

"They gave us deliverance."

"Still, after years of abuse from the Nazis and now our experiences with the Canadian *Special Ops* battalion, we were all left emotionally raw and shaken. We were still afraid. We believed anything could still happen in a world tipped toward insanity."

"Then we heard tanks rumbling down the road toward us before we could see them. We believed the Germans were coming back to take revenge upon the Canadians and on us."

"*We would all surely die.*"

"My father tried to herd us all back to the cellar. My sister, stopping dead in her tracks, pointed—the tanks flew American flags. The men driving the tanks and sitting astride the guns were more Canadians and their berets were bathed in sunshine. This different group of men wore smiles! They were smiling at the very air around them!"

"I remember thinking, 'This is joy!' "

"We had heard that the Canadians could not afford to build their own tanks. So that rumour was true! We hid by the broken windows of our homes. It took hours before we smiled back from broken panes, then slowly we emerged. These men were

Canadians but no longer the somber special ops who had flushed out the Nazis hiding in our homes. These men distributed food! And *blankets*! And JOY!"

"Those unsmiling Canadians had been our saviours after all! Where were they? We learned from this new batch of Canadians that they had moved on to the next town— where again they would be the somber saviours. The smiles would come later, with these new men, for our family and friends living there."

"The Canadians saved us."

"We had prayed that the Allies would end this nightmare. We had prayed that God would deliver us from evil—that He was not dead."

"God *was not* dead!"

The relief and joy that my mother's words emitted should have been in my father's words. He was only capable of, "We were free and we were alive." That is the difference between shades of black and the brightness of a rainbow. Neither of my parents lost those shades in their lifetime and I inherited both, although God was dead for one and very alive for the other.

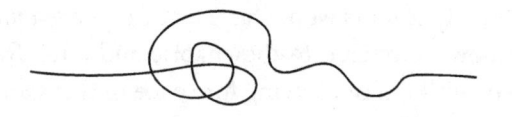

One Unit

My husband had gone fishing. I was by myself in a body-hugging Muskoka chair. I was thinking of the paradox my parents represented as I sat on the deck outside our cabin in the north country of Ontario. The aloneness of our autumn holiday suited me, to a tee, this day. Colour surrounded me. Deepest blue was the water beneath my feet, under the deck. Gradually, it merged with black water as I glanced up toward the far shore. Bright yellows, reds, and pine greens reflected, floating across the black water. Like my mother's brightness had washed over my father's darkness. As I lifted my eyes some more, the colours burst forth against the bright, light blue sky. God's work enveloped me in its warmth although the air was cooling in the autumn winds. It was glorious!

For once, I was at peace with my thoughts. That gave me time to daydream about a whole, healthy adytum. It was certainly a long journey to find that sacred place within me. But I had felt a sense of awe and reverence for the privilege of being alive more frequently of late. I guess that is why I felt so serene at this moment.

I sat thinking about how intricately my life was coupled to family in both the past and the present. My eyes teared up as I reminisced about memories I had been struggling with for my father's memoir; I felt emotional as each memory cranked open yet another set of long-ago experiences. Yet I wiped away my tears when I thought of our recent summer holiday, here at the cabin, with our children and grandchildren. My parents would have loved that *one-unit* experience. My solitude now, compared to the chaotic and often frenzied week we'd had then, with ten of us vying for space in this same cabin, was just like the contrast between my parents' natures.

I had brought my laptop up with me for moments like this. But which was the recollection with which to begin my work? Should I even contemplate my father's memoirs here in this idyllic spot? I made a conscious choice to begin this day's journey with bright thoughts. Our family's summer holiday had been only weeks ago and I could still hear the laughter! Here was definitely the starting place. I drifted into memory with a huge smile on my face.

"Families do live on as one!" I could not help a quick glance toward heaven.

***

Our Family Holiday

Sunshine filtered between puffy, white clouds which brought momentary bouts of cooling shade from the sizzling sun. A warm breeze drifted toward us from the pines behind the cabin carrying our scent to the beavers outside their den on the far side of the island-spotted river. Loud laughter erupted from the beach as our two oldest grandsons, Sam and little Willy, entered the water before they had even gone into the cabin upon their arrival. No bathing suits required! The boat had pulled up to the dock. They had somehow emerged from between loads of camping gear, without help, and disappeared.

As the rest of us busied ourselves unloading the boat, for the third time, Sam and Willy's mother, Amy, yelled out in annoyance, "You guys have all of your clothes on! And *no* life jackets! Get out of the water. *Now!*"

I wandered over to the other end of the deck, beside the beach, to make sure the boys stripped down to their underwear before putting on the lifejackets which I carried. I was too late. They were already naked. Clothes lay strewn across the beach, and they were in heaven. I tossed each of them a piece of survival equipment.

Ah . . . to be seven and four years old and in the lake on the first day of vacation! Still, they needed safety gear! And maybe some underwear.

In the distance, we heard sea-doos racing over the big bay just out of sight, around the small peninsula next to the cabin. It prompted the boys to leave the water for a moment, just long enough to beg Grandpa for a tube ride behind the boat.

"It has to be later guys. Oli and baby Abe need a nap before we do anything noisy," my husband told them. "Auntie Laura needs you to try to be quiet for a bit."

"You guys get off the dock now. We don't want to knock you into the lake with unloading. You're in the way!" their dad, our son Mark, told his boys. "Go catch frogs."

They were up to their knees in mud before Mark had turned his back.

"Where's the freezer? It's gone!" My daughter held baby Abe while two-year-old Oli ran toward the dock. "Oli! No life jacket! Remember? Just stay with me. Nap time!"

"No!" Oli practiced his favourite two-year-old word. His only word so far!

I had to hide my smile. He had learned that he could say "no" only the week before and the twinkle in his eyes as he said it brought back memories of my children's first word. "No" of course!

"The old freezer is in the shed. You can try to stuff more into the little one under the fridge," I prompted. "All the prime real estate in there is gone though! You may be in the shed this time." It was always a chore getting everything we brought for a week, for ten people, into the cabin's meager storage space. Still, it was all part of the adventure. I took hold of Oli's hand and guided him toward his cousins and the frogs. At least that would give Laura and her husband Jon a chance to ease into their little reserved space in the cabin. Laura did always seem to squeeze her family in, no matter how crowded it got, but her brother never stopped teasing her about how different things used to be.

"Laura, remember the roll goblin? Is he still alive and well?"

"Shut up, Mark. I swear if you start poking me right now, I will throw you in the lake! I need to get these boys down for a nap!"

"You used to love me to pinch your neck roll until the goblin popped out? What?"

Laura had taken a swing at her brother as he went for the little mole on her neck. But their laughter brought back memories of long trips in the car when she had not loved his teasing quite so much. All we would hear on the drive up was, "Mom, Dad, he's touching me! Tell him not to touch me!" Then when I looked back, Mark would be sitting innocently looking out of the car window. Ah... the harmonious past—it made me sigh.

About an hour later, Oli and baby Abe finally fell asleep.

Unpacked and ready to have our holiday, Laura, Amy, and I stood in the grass behind the cabin and caught the fresh scent of pine sap rolling out of the forest surrounding us. A large V of Canada geese honked by overhead.

"Isn't it great to be back?" Laura whispered.

"Yes! Especially when all the boys are busy fishing off the dock! And the babies are sleeping! It is so quiet now," Amy added restfully. The smell of BBQ ribs brought us back to the small deck in back of the cabin and the huge dinner we were preparing.

"It is always so peaceful here; Grandma and Grandpa would have loved it, eh?" Laura whispered.

"Yeah. This place would certainly have brought them joy," I whispered back. I hugged both girls to me as we shared a memory of family members long past. Amy had lost her father years ago as well and she knew the feelings we spoke of. We always took a moment to remember those who could not join us in the fun—

"Let the games begin!" Laura broke the mood. "Supper's ready!"

The stampede which followed that announcement washed away all hints of nostalgia. The week, which was always deemed too short, proceeded to become one of the rowdiest ever. Card tournaments that went on into the night, campfires that burned with all the colours of the rainbow thanks to some packets of "stuff" added to the logs, big meals, tube rides, and fishing trips, and mostly jumping off the raft into the lake a million times per day filled our lives with almost too much joy. The boundaries of separate families could be easily broken here. We lived as one big, happy family.

The last morning was always filled with every one of us busy trying to pack away memories to last us with laughter until the following jaunt next summer. I awoke that morning to the sounds of every member of our one big family trying to make breakfast at the same time. My husband, happy as a pig in shit, ran the kitchen like a pro. Everyone had a chore, even the boys. Sam and Willy stirred big bowls of biscuit dough. Oli was manning the dishcloth—to clean up the inevitable spills of course. Little Abe screamed his hunger from the highchair next to his father. All was well with the world.

Luscious scents floated into my room. Family gossip drifted into my ears. I peeked out into the Loony Room, as we called the living room area of the cottage. The walls were dark blue, like the water just outside the floor-to-ceiling windows overlooking the lake. The pictures hanging on the walls depicted loons in every aspect of their lives on the lake. Some had fish in their mouths, others carried babies on their backs. All represented peace for me. The kitchen noises drowned them out now, but loons could be heard crooning at all times of the day and night, here at the cabin.

Loons calling were what I remembered most when I left this place. Loons called for me when I wanted to feel at peace, although it seemed out of my reach at times. When I was at my desk, remembering, I could sometimes hear them call. Funny though, how loons could represent both peace *and* the turmoil I heard in the kitchen as I awoke fully that last morning.

I walked out into the tumult.

This place and these people were most certainly heaven. Thank you, God!

* * *

My father would have said to my mother, "Mama, look what we started!" Their lives were always complete when their family gathered around them, as is mine.

Joy of family is an inheritance never to be outweighed.

Memories tell our stories. Sharing memories reminds us of how far we've come. And the future holds dreams of where we still hope to be. But throughout our lives, family is the centre. My father told me so!

Now as I basked in my solitary Muskoka chair, I glanced toward heaven again. The haunted call of a loon arched across the distance from the big bay. It rolled to my ears over the dark water and its colours, to seal my thoughts with peace.

"These thoughts are most precious to me, Dad. They make me a whole person."

These thoughts help me to rebuild my adytum.

* * *

"Write about something extremely important to you," he'd said.

> After three days, after our liberation, we had to get ready for our big trip home—to Belgium! Hopefully to see everyone alive—again—that was in the back of our heads. We stole a small cart to transport whatever the six of us wanted to take along—after all, we were six best friends, bound together and did not want to leave each other. Two would push, two would pull, one would steer, one would rest—that's how we started home, filled with courage.

My mother's and my father's stories never meshed as one. They were the stories of two lives and were told for two separate purposes. One was told to make us hate and the other to bring back love. After my parents left me alone with only their stories to remember them by, the stories became an unending stream-of-consciousness memory loop. In my mind, my mother won this confusing dispute, although I sometimes felt tugged and pulled in both directions. When I was much younger, their stories somehow became my story. At times, I felt that my own life was an intrusion upon a past that I believed I had lived. Many times, I wondered if this spell I found myself woven into was stealing my childhood. Then I realized that my life was, in part, those memories, and I grasped at them like manna.

* * *

I understand that my life is an intricate mesh of kin, glued by complex relationships with those people that I love. I was thinking about that fact as snowflakes drifted heavily outside my office window. Thick, white clumps tumbled down wetly like the very manna from heaven, bringing to life my own simile. Each complex snowflake that fell was like a separate piece of my past that landed hard against my mind. It was almost Christmas. There was not even a month left before St. Nick would ride the winds to deliver his gifts and blessings. My grandchildren were busy writing lists while I struggled to write their story.

Somehow my thoughts seemed to gather in corners like the snow; my mind was clogged and frozen over with multidirectional fluff. My moods were bleaker than the weather at times. Snowfall can be uplifting but the grey days and black nights left me feeling directionless. The few short hours of daylight illuminating the snowpack did nothing for my diminishing spirits.

What could I possibly tell my grandchildren that would spark their interest in times past? Especially when they were so busy with school plays and, believe me, a continually changing letter to Santa!

"You ready for a walk in the snow?" My husband stuck his head in the door, a huge grin on his face. He always knew when I needed a break from my labour.

"I am sooo very ready! Let's go get wet!"

The wet snow stuck to our toques, coats, boots; we became snowball people. Soon we could no longer see the separate flakes. Everything was a brilliant white. The silence of our walk through the woods, in deep snow, muffled all sounds except for the rubbing of the snow pants between our thighs. It was a cheerful, childish sound that made us both laugh.

"You won't believe what I read the other day," Rudy announced. "Some scientist actually did a study on how happy just walking under trees makes people!"

"Really? And how happy should this make us?" I grinned.

"Well, they determined that it makes people as happy as they are on Christmas morning!"

"Christmas morning? Really?"

"Yup! Kind of like that old story you told me about your mother at Christmas time. The one about how her father always came up with something new to entertain his eight children and anyone else who happened by on Christmas day."

I gaped at him. "Wow! You are brilliant, my good man!"

"What? How brilliant?"

"I'll let you know after chapter six!"

And there we had it. My husband had just solved my every question. My mother's stories! I tossed a snowball that knocked his hat off. Then I ploughed through the snow trying to dodge his missile. Even this winter weather, with its grey, ominous clouds which promised more and more snow overnight, was something to rejoice in now.

That very afternoon I scribbled down my mother's St. Nicholas story for my grandchildren. I wrote it as she told it to me:

St. Nicholas

"VaVa, my father, once convinced us that St. Nicholas really did exist when we had said we didn't believe. He insisted that some tracks on our roof had been made by Santa, his reindeer, and their sleigh. He bundled us all up, all eight of us, and took us to the yard. There he pointed up and showed us the "tracks." Indeed, there were footprints like those of tiny reindeer—we didn't know what those looked like. And there were definitely boot prints—small ones. Plus, there were skid marks where the "sleigh" had come to a halt. For years after that episode, every child on our street believed in St. Nicholas. During that time, before the war, dreams did come true. Another Christmas, VaVa ran into our kitchen, gathered us all, and breathlessly told us that Santa's sleigh had just tipped over in the market square. Needless to say, we all ran to the square in our PJs and slippers. However, that time he said that Santa had simply cleaned up the mess and gone on his way before we, slow children, could get to the market. We all still strongly believed. VaVa made childhood magic. His magic consisted of a pair of children's boots on a rope, and a stray cat who, once thrown onto the roof, walked a bit and slid off the edge. We never thought to look down at the cat tracks below the eaves. The magic was very real."

The stories of St. Nicholas and his sleigh urged generations of our family to believe; I told my children and they told theirs. The magic lives—as long as stray cats roam our neighbourhoods!

The charm of my mother's stories was that they bound each generation of our family with the next. The telling of them always made family members, who were far away in Belgium, seem near. That was because we knew those distant relatives told the same stories every year at Christmas, as we did.

* * *

I received a text the other day from my daughter, Laura. It was a picture of her oldest son, Oli, playing in the snow. His toque was askew and his grin infectious. But it was the snowflakes mixed into his dark curls that made me cry. He looked positively angelic, framed as he was by snow-laden evergreens. My arms ached to hold him. My heart splintered across the distance separating us. My daughter and her family lived hours away, in Kincardine.

Then my tears washed a memory from a forgotten corner of my soul. I recognized the pain of separation I felt through the mirror of time.

Every few months, my parents would receive letters from my grandparents in Belgium. One year, near Christmas time, I found my mother in tears. When I rushed toward her, she jumped out of her chair and gently pulled me into her arms. She did not stop crying. Her sobs shook both her and me while I desperately guessed at the *something terrible* that had come from afar. It had to be something so horrendous to my mother that it made her division from her family, in Belgium, intolerable. And it made contact with me imperative.

Cancer had taken hold of my grandmother. This made my mother's choice, to live thousands of miles from her, soul-searing.

Separation from family is damaging and heart wrenching. That very fact made me realize that the stories that bind can build a love that never dies, that those stories can solidify the unit.

And those stories give joy, like Christmas morning!

> We had to travel about 1000 km back to Belgium. It was easier said than done—that we would go home quickly. But we would make the best of it! We left Halberstadt, which had been our prison, on April 13, 1945...

For my father and his friends, I imagined that it must have felt like Christmas morning! But my father could only record that they, "would make the best of it."

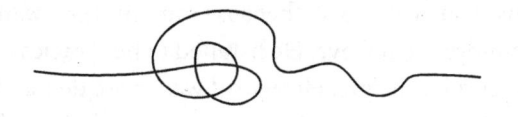

Survival Guide

I have been described as a hard person. While I disagree with this assessment, I can understand why someone might think me an inflexible person. After all, I inherited my father's stubborn streak. I know my parenting style developed from some rigid philosophies. I am only now realizing that I can relate the way I learned to parent to how my father taught me to survive life's challenges. He taught that what we think can outweigh the corporeal world around us. And his lessons included ideas about inner strength being more important than physical abilities. Another of his beliefs included that unwavering courage can conquer anything the world throws at us. These mottoes were my father's Survival Guide. He did not give lectures or speeches; he taught by example. I learned from watching him face each of his life challenges with determination, grit, and resilience. I recognize that I have not been a perfect parent. I have, however, dutifully stuck to my father's hard-earned survivor's guidelines, though adapted by my mother's love. It was the only way I could love my children the most.

To have heard my father speak, it would not always have been clear that those were his maxims. But they were very much a part of his unschooled philosophy. That he even had a philosophy would have surprised many who knew him. But he did—it was his pure philosophy of endurance. His was a set of values which could apply to all of our lives if only we cared to absorb his principles. I applied those principles to my own life.

He believed in Santa only because our mother wanted him to allow their children to believe. He listened to her fancies only because he loved her and her magic. His world was more demanding and difficult to grasp because his magic was a lost thing he was always trying to recover, for her. I am the fanciful one in our home. My husband is more practical but he loves my musings. He loves me.

We kept the magic alive for our children even though we both worked away from home. Unexpectedly, a relative, who happened to have the luxury of being a stay-at-home mom, accused both my husband and me of not being there for our children. She believed their babysitters, my parents, were bringing up our children for us. She told us we were being negligent. Of course, I took that personally while my husband shrugged it off as the ravings of a lunatic. She made me feel like a dishonourable sort of mother because I chose to work full time.

Me? Hard? No.

Determined? Gritty? Resilient? Most definitely.

How I prayed for a chance to have a choice but, for the support of all, our family needed the money. Needing two incomes was a common social ailment of the times back in the 80s. That illness is still a part of our society. My children went to spend parts of some days with their grandparents. My parents were at relative peace during this time in their lives. During the turbulent times of our young household, the lives of my daughter and my son could only be enhanced by contact with their grandparents' tranquility.

I left them, yes. And I cannot describe how much that hurt, still hurts, especially whenever any mother's time away from her children is pointed out within my hearing, quite brutally, by people who will never understand her sacrifice.

I truly believed that the time spent with their grandparents would saturate my children with a part of their story which I could not tell. The mixing of generations left my children with more than a memory of their past. I felt that, while I worked, my children were enriching their lives with the fullness of impressions which only their grandma and grandpa could impart.

My children, now years later, have fully partaken of a chronicle made up of more than each of our separate lives. They possess a thorough knowledge of their own history. Hearing their grandparents' stories firsthand, gave them insight into the experiences of lives lived long before theirs.

I believe that grandchildren spending time with grandparents is not the negligent behavior of uncaring parents, as my assailant would have had me believe. It is the completion of a circle of love as old as time. Those who do not understand have somehow missed the very point of life.

In order to endure the hurt inflicted by this woman's unthinking comment, I resorted to my father's wisdom and explained away her accusations to myself as I have explained them here. I allowed my positive belief about my parenting methods to outweigh her opinion. I allowed my inner strength to filter through my weakness and doubt after what she had attacked me with. And lastly, Dad, I was brave enough to never suffer that woman in my life again, ever.

Looking at my children now, as adults, I'm reassured that I have indeed lived to create a rich family heritage for them; not everyone is fortunate enough to possess this. I transferred to them a strong will to live with true grit and resilience, as my father did for me. I am sure they are likely to survive traumatic episodes in their lives better than most. I survived. And, eventually, my confidence did too.

With focused determination I taught my children to be masters of their own fates. I needed to trust my decisions rather than fear that my methods did my children harm. In my understanding, this confidence is crucial to teaching children. I wanted to be able to feel that I had been conscientious in my choices for my beloved children. I needed to feel that I was adequate to the challenges of raising good people. I did not ever desire the pain of being found wanting in any way. Still, this brutal attacker found my weakness. She attacked my love for my children. I hope other parents are spared the pain I felt when my tormentor belittled me. Because parents are human. My parents were human, my husband and I are human. But both of us and our children possess inner strength beyond my father's wildest dreams. Thank you, Dad.

* * *

I am captivated by a vision of life as narrative; others, I am sure, compose life narratives as they go along, zigzagging this way and that, without a firm base upon which to build a story. Some may call this *flying by the seat of your pants*. I need more concrete foundations for my stories. Who is to say which is wrong? My husband and I wanted to feel that we had reached into the hearts of our children, as our parents had done for us. We wanted to touch their thoughts, even if only because we had been teaching no one else but them. I felt my parents' hands on my shoulders each time I taught my children about the narrative of their past. My father's philosophies were in the story-line of his endurance, in his ability to survive. I learned them as best I could. I taught them to my children through my parents' stories but I interspersed those stories with my mother's leaven. I simply could not subject them to the trauma I had endured.

> Our first day we left Halberstadt on our way to Strobeek, Danstedt, where we stayed the night—after only 15 km. On the second day—Saturday, April 14, Danstedt, we left at 8:30 am. We traveled 25 km that day through Heudeler, Langeln, Wasserleben, Beisel, Schauwen, Osterwieck, and Vienenburg, where we stayed overnight.

It was typical for my father to focus on the business at hand—getting home. He did not mention in his written memoirs that he weighed less than he had at age twelve, at the beginning of his journey. He mentioned tidbits such as this only when he could no longer hold back the rage he carried through the rest of his life. He then told of atrocities which darkened my world forever. He counted his ribs each night on the journey home while he ate everything he could find to assuage his hunger. Garbage—sometimes they ate garbage. I feel guilty thinking "I'm starving" when I haven't eaten for a few hours. *Garbage...*

> On the third day, Sunday, April 15 at 7:30 am, we left Vienenburg on our way to another bunch of cities—Goslar, Astfeld, Langelheim, and Seesen. We stayed in Seesen over night—we had gone 33 km. On the fourth day, Monday, April 16 at 8:30 am, we left Seesen to go to Ildehausen, Echte, and Imshausen where we stayed overnight. We had gone 20 km.

Garbage. My father had eaten garbage. And to the day he died he gulped his food. When he ate, he stuffed so much into his mouth that he could not close his lips. In his memoir when he told of his journey out of hell in his brutally straightforward way—leaving out what I already knew from his tirades and what I share with you here—my mother would interject her leaven. She turned those darknesses into quiet remembrances of a life lived instead of merely survived. That was why he loved her so much.

Leaven

> "Your grandfather raced pigeons. It was his hobby. He and all of his friends were in fierce competition. Sometimes the beer would disappear so fast on race day that some flyers would miss the returning racers and forfeit their prize. All was taken in stride since it was fun and they all felt they had won when every bird returned home safely."

> "One time, your grandfather took his racers to France on the back of his bike. In fact, all of his friends drove with him—each with a basket full of racers on their rickety bikes. They left their birds with the competition authorities in France and returned home as quickly as their peddling could carry them. There, they

would all drink beer and wait for the birds to be released to fly home. Our neighbour missed the return of his winning bird because he did not see it return to its nest. A bit too much beer that day! VaVa removed the band from his first bird when it returned to its roost. He figured he had not won so he clocked the band and set the time that the bird had returned. He was in no hurry going to the officials to record his bird's time. When he finally got there, he was surprised to find that his neighbour had not clocked his winning bird. They gave the prize to VaVa and he and his friends went to find out what the owner of the actual winning bird was thinking, or rather, what he was drinking!"

"The grandmother clock, that your grandfather won that day, hung in our kitchen until I brought it here after your grandmother's death. The clock has been pledged from mother to daughter since then."

The clock hangs in my living room to this day. My mother left it to me. I will leave it to my daughter. The story will linger forever. We called it the story of the first second prize. The lesson? Never drink too much while your birds are flying. It's funny because it is like the lesson about never counting your chickens before they hatch—nothing is lost in translation.

My father's black and white imaging is enhanced by my mother's telling of the war events in her life. All of her life was told in technicolour. There is the difference between my mother and my father—my mother described life while my father experienced a sudden death of spirit at the hands of his captors. My mother brought him back to life with her living reconstructions. And with her sharp tongue.

And suddenly, the gloomy, grey-black clouds outside my window this day seem less ominous. Christmas is almost here, after all.

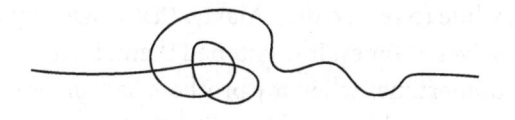

The Leavening

Christmas came and went in a blur of activity and with its passing came my annual desire for spring. But Ontario winters can leave one with such a longing for a very, very long time. January, February, March, and even April can quadruple the craving for something more to life than snow and slush, winter coats, and layers of warm clothing. March was marching on slowly with no hope of sunshine in the forecast as I gazed out of my window in hope of inspiration.

The one thing I realized was that there is no wrong impression to be taken from my mother's stories. Hers are also stories of survival. The stories are what she thought of during her darkest hours, during times designed to kill the soul. During her time spent surviving a war that she was too young to comprehend, and again later, during times when my father's nightmares tapped her spirit.

When my father's parents passed away, he slipped into darkness. I remember his voice in the night saying continuously, "They were my family."

My mother could be brutal when she needed to save him and save herself.

"*We* are your family, you fool!" she whispered in a hiss. These words were echoed in the darkness around me; they thought I slept. My brothers were heavy sleepers, I guess, I was not. Perhaps this affected their ability to understand the whole history and its effects on our parents. Not everyone's father wakes up choked on a scream;

it took me a while to realize that. Maybe that is why my brothers distanced themselves at times. It frightened them. It frightened me. But I remember dinnertimes when my brothers had all moved away. The only sounds at that table were the sounds of chewing and swallowing. I would begin talking at times like this just to keep my parents entertained. My adolescent stories sounded superficial then, even to my own ears.

It irks me that I cannot remember anything that I had said during those times. I'm sure my stories all revolved around me and my life—after all, I was a teenager. The lengthy renditions of the events of my day would at least ease the monotony of our silent meals and I *do* remember my parents would smile from time to time. I smiled at the thought that I had cheered them—that was comforting.

Today I had my office window cracked open to replace some of the stale winter air held captive in our home. As I sat musing about my ability to soothe my parents, the smell of someone's fireplace drifted across the slushy snow and into my imagination. Fireplaces and wood smoke always took me to Kincardine and walks there with my daughter and her little ones. Everyone has a fireplace in that town! In March, they still had two feet of snow on the ground!

Yes. Wood smoke makes me think of my grandchildren, be it in Kincardine or in my son's backyard just around the corner from us. My grandchildren are the reason I write this history in the first place. This story will teach them the unerring love of family.

Grandchildren spending time with grandparents is the completion of a circle as old as time. Sometimes that circle remains incomplete when it should not be so. Maybe my brothers did not want to frighten their children. But the history needs to be known to complete their knowledge of themselves, to complete their knowledge of love.

My father worded his love for my mother best, "She left me now. I want to go with her."

My mother's hand still rested lifelessly in his when he mouthed those words which burned my heart to cinders. The family history nearly perished in those ashes. It feels hollow when you cannot fill such a void, not even with copious amounts of love for a lonely father.

It felt impossible to fix myself or to fix him. I heard his words at my mother's side and experienced the adhesiveness of family slip out of my grasp.

* * *

I remember being thirteen years old and learning that I could hurt someone so extremely that the emotion had a sight, sound, and even a physical feel to it. I learned that heartache was a living blade that can tear into a person's life when least expected. I learned that, being razor sharp, the blade could be carelessly wielded by a cruel lapse in a teenager's judgment.

My father had worked late that night. He came home to his reheated meal, over-tired and eager for some quiet time with his two favourite girls.

I, on the other hand, was unwilling to give him rest until I had my way.

"Awe come on Dad; everyone is wearing jeans! I am so out of date it's ridiculous!" I whined.

"I said no. No girl of mine is going to wear those hippie rags! And as for the party you asked to go to on the weekend, at Sandy's house, forget that too. You are too young to even think of going to parties with boys!"

"Mom! Say something! Save me here! I am going to die an old maid!"

"Dad already gave you your answer, Mary. That's the end of it! Leave me out of it!" my mom warned. "And stop asking for things we will not allow!"

"Good God!" I swore. "Neither of you understands anything! It isn't 1940 anymore you know!"

I had stood up, ready to stomp out of the dining room, before I noticed the dead silence behind me.

I heard the fork lightly hit the side of his plate. Then I saw my father's face. The agony I saw reflected in his eyes was a sight that forced me to sit down again.

When I managed to look up, I saw his overfull mouth working to swallow. I had stolen the will to eat from a man who had had to swallow garbage.

I heard the laboured, dry swallow next. It was a forlorn and hollow sound so slow that it seemed to pass into forever. The sound still haunts my heart to this day.

My mother's hard slap sent me reeling in my chair and I remember thinking, "She has never hit me before—this is bad." It put a physical hurt to the emotional torture I had just caused them both.

How thoughtless could I be? How cruel? How self-centred?

What had I just done in anger?

1940?

That was the year my mother was thirteen and had faced off with Nazi soldiers who would not have hesitated to abuse her in any way, because they thought they owned her. It was a year she would never have thought to ask for anything for herself because her family had nothing, not even enough food. That had been the year she had helped to hide one of her brothers from the enemy soldiers. It was a time during which she feared for the lives of her five other brothers, her parents, and her little sister *every day*.

1940 was the year my father had worked forced eighteen-hour days for the Nazis. He had been working for the third Reich for two years already. He had been eighteen when he started. That year, he was twenty. He had no freedom then, no choices, no decisions; he had only the work he was forced to do and not enough food to eat. He hadn't even had clothes on his back for much of that year!

Now my father stood and left the table with food still on his plate. I noticed desolately that he had not even eaten half of his supper. He had walked away, after that pain-filled swallow, with tears in his eyes and his mouth still overfull.

Remorseful does not even begin to describe how I felt seeing him walk away. I then wished that my mother had used her closed fist to hit me!

Still, after time, they forgave me.

Still they loved me.

I did not deserve their love, ungrateful brat that I was.
So I never wore jeans. And I never went to parties growing up.
I do not feel like I missed anything.
But, to this day, shame haunts me and reminds me of my callousness.
The cutting edge of our heartache had sliced to the quick.
Children can be cruel.
I had been cruel.
That was the day that I learned never to be malicious again. Ever.
Yes. I remember being thirteen.

* * *

At thirteen and a half, I ended a cold war within my home. It had been months since the epic tragedy through which I had caused my own downfall from grace. During those months, I had racked my brain for ways to repair the rift caused by my irresponsible behaviour.

One evening, my father worked late again. I asked my mother not to reheat the meal she had lovingly set aside for him. I wanted to make him his meal—a sandwich. I sliced the homemade bread, I shaved a piece of the dinner ham. I slathered mayonnaise over the two slices of fragrant bread and tucked the ham inside. I filled a mason jar with cold brewed coffee and silently set it before the man to whom I then vowed, "*I will never* hurt you again."

My dad picked up the plate, came to sit next to me, and wrapped one arm around my shivering shoulders. He took a huge bite of his sandwich. It was a bite too big for his mouth but he still managed to smile around it.

I felt like a blanket of purple hyacinth had bloomed around my heart. As an emblem of forgiveness, the flower meant new life to me. My father knew I had been sorrowful for a long while with no true means to apologize. I closed my eyes and envisioned us both, surrounded by a field of purple, sweet-smelling blooms, as I rested my head on my father's strong shoulder. I listened to him chew and swallow. It was the happiest sound in the world to my ears!

And I cried.

When I could speak, I told him that I was determined to learn how to cook *all* of his favourite foods for him. And since then, I have cooked to show people how much I love them. For me, cooking is an expression of true love.

Thank you, Dad.

From that time on, my mother joyfully taught me to express myself through food. We cooked and baked every day. It was glorious!

We never mentioned my disgrace, not once.

Then one day, I asked her to tell me the tale of her brother, my Uncle Alfons. He was the brother she and her parents had hidden from the Nazis, her youngest brother.

She smiled at me, made tea, and then we settled in for a story.

***

Hiding

"Some men in 1940, like your uncle Alfons, were hiding out during the war. The Belgian government had sent them to their fates without weapons when the Nazis invaded their country. Our country's officials figured that becoming captives was better than dying in a battle against a powerful neighbour. They surely had no right to decide such a fate for so many. But those were frightening times. And some men hid because of the decisions of others."

"Fons hid for part of a year in an old car that had rusted in the back field of a neighbour's farm for years. It was eight kilometers from our house but he could travel back and forth at night through the lanes connecting the properties. We fed him at night. When winter came, we moved him into our own attic. It was still cold up there but we could give him clothes and blankets. One night, we thought the Nazis had broken in and found him—we feared for all of our lives. There was a horrible racket, a commotion we thought was a deadly struggle. But then my brother rushed into the kitchen from his hiding place, in the middle of the night, without his pants on!"

"The battle had been with a rat! Our cat, whom Fons had elected as his protector against the attic mice, had lost an epic battle with a huge rat before succumbing to its wounds. Then the vicious rat had run at my brother and up his loose-fitting pants. Apparently, the rat had felt the cold in the attic as well! Funny in hindsight but just imagine! Your grandfather and my brother, Fons, had to go up there and kill the thing. I was young and I mourned my cat. Your grandmother reminded me that it was better to lose a cat, than a brother to the war."

"You see," she ended, "all thirteen-year-olds can be thoughtless."

*　*　*

My mother mostly recounted the lighter side of their very serious situation. She had been young and hopeful as all children are. But when the war ended, she was eighteen and even her inner child had become cynical. Her lighter stories were kept for needy times in our family—when my father had become depressed or one of us had reacted poorly to one of his episodes of raging hatred. Other times, her horror of the events of WWII could be felt by everyone in the room. Empathic or not, I shuddered at her relation of events during her teenage years. Some most profound memories of those years in her life involved a woman I had met only once, a year before she died. The history of my grandmother, Moe Melis as we called her, was what erupted from the hidden recesses of my mother's heart. I learned from her that being a teenager is not the same for any two people.

The Beating

"The German soldiers lived in our village during the occupation. They were told to be good to the people, for the most part.

They wanted our cooperation. They wanted intelligence, information from the underground. They knew some of the people in our village could be turned. They had used people in other villages. They wanted to use our home as an intelligence centre. Moe Melis said, 'No!' Then she blocked the way of a minor officer trying to bring in radio equipment. She argued with him that she had two daughters in the house, and she did not want any more danger to surround them than the Nazis had already brought with them. She did not want the war inside her home."

"He did not understand her Belgian dialect."

"She was beaten to the ground by the young Nazi officer. Her face bloodied and split open to the bone. I ran to pick her up and take her inside. My mother was broken and defeated before my eyes and the piece of scum that did it just walked away. I screamed for help, and it came in the form of a high-ranking Nazi officer. The young brute's superior."

"Apparently, the higher-ranking officer told my mother, the younger man had not listened to the same orders as his compatriots. He had been ordered to treat all inhabitants of the village with kindness, to be good to them. And to be especially good to my parents since the Nazis had really wanted a base in our home, a central location which would suit their purposes well, as spies. Now instead, the young officer was beaten to within an inch of his life. He was dragged, bleeding and delirious, some bones at odd angles, for my mother and me and my sister to observe. Another location was to be found, one less conspicuous in circumstance. My sister and I were sick at the sight of both our mother's injuries and the young man's agony. But at that time, we felt he deserved it nonetheless."

"I was set to work that night in our café, slinging beer to the regular Nazi soldiers sent to make amends to our parents. Your grandfather was a suspected member of the underground and they still thought they could turn him with companionship and beer. They did not know the depth of the hatred simmering beneath the surface of your grandfather's 'hospitality.' It was the same hatred I found in your father when I met him."

She later told me it was the same hatred she had felt, at the time, for their captors since the night of her mother's abuse at their hands. It was a hatred she never shared with any of her children more than this once. Why I was the chosen child to bear it witness, I cannot say. But I am glad she let it out, just once.

* * *

I cannot forget one particular snowy afternoon when I was home from school. It was a snow day. It was the first day of the Blizzard of 1977, in the Niagara Region. It was the blizzard Erno Rossi wrote about in his book, *White Death*. No one dared to brave that storm. So my parents were home too. My mother decided early in the day that some of her lighter stories might entertain us until the storm passed.

Party Time

"Slinging beer after the liberation, that was a party! Everyone was drunk. Everyone was happy. Everyone drowned their worries that night. The only one complaining was my little sister. She was fifteen and had been forced into a dress she hated. It was a dress that fit tightly over her belly which miraculously had not shrunk during the war. There was a particular Canadian soldier she had wanted to notice her. But not in that dress! Funny times! It is not like the dress she was wearing would have made any difference on that day! Teenagers! They can elevate the trivial!"

* * *

Whenever my mother spoke of the liberation, it always took my father back to his own struggles to free himself and his friends from their horror. That snowy afternoon was no different. He could not let her tell the happy tale without interjecting the reality of his ever-present hell. That day, he recited it from memory; later he recorded it for me. I took the story from his memoir:

> On the fifth day, Tuesday, April 17, we left Imshausen at 12:30 and continued our walk in shoes that swished with our own blood. We walked anyway, home. We walked through Langenholtensen, Northeim, Sudheim, Nortem, Hardenberg, and into Angerstein where we stayed overnight. We had made it only 18 km that day. We were sore and tired and our blisters had opened again. We had been wearing these shoes a very, very long time.

My mother's efforts to distract our father were not always successful. My father would continue his stories from where he had left off each time she stopped speaking. I saw his eyes glaze over sometimes when she spoke. I knew he was trying to listen but that his demons were stronger than her attempt to abolish them. He went on:

> On the sixth day, Wednesday, April 18, we left Angerstein at 7:15 am. We limped to Gotingen, through Bosenden, Weende, Cane, Rosdorf, Abengershausen, Lemshausen, Vollerrode, Abariengarten, Daklingrode and finally stayed overnight in Atzenhausen. We had gone 29 km. It was a grueling march, going home.

I can still hear my mother snapping her fingers until she got my attention. She told me that she and her sister had sung in the church choir. They had also sung in the school choir. I suddenly realized why my mother sounded so good when she sang to us. She had a voice!

It was a voice none of us had inherited—but it was still part of our history. Maybe someday our children's children would sing again.

That icy afternoon, my father did not care to hear about my mother's singing. Doggedly, he returned to *his* story:

> It was the seventh day of our freedom and it was Thursday, April 19. We left Atzenhausen at 8:30 am to walk to Han-Munden where we found out we had to wait for three hours. We were not patient to wait; home is where we were going and where we wanted to be. But after three hours, we were able to cross the Werra in a boat. On the other side we walked on to Lutterberg. We were so anxious to get home but we needed to rest. We stayed there, in Lutterberg. Only 18 km from our last stop. It was beginning to feel like a fool's errand, to walk every day and get nowhere.

Our dog came bounding into the room and my mother took an opportunity to change the subject, again.

Bob

"Do you know how Bob got his name? Well, he is not the first dog in this family named Bob! We had a watchdog during the war and *his* name was Bob. He would bark at the bombs and the gunfire for hours. I would calm him down by singing to him. My sister used to say, 'Our Bob, ten hours from here to the canon folk and you hear all of it.' He was a Belgian Tervuren and he was very smart. He made me feel safe during the war because he was so kind to me and protective of me. When we got a dog here, I asked your father if we could name him Bob. If his name was Bob, I knew he would keep us safe."

Our family has always had a Bob. It became a tradition which we all loved. Each dog lived in remembrance of my mother's protector during WWII. I always thought there could be no better tradition and no better name for a dog.

The *Bob* distraction was a much needed one for my mother and me—but not for my father. He resolutely hung on to his narrative until my mother's story was finished. He needed to get to a certain point in his reminiscences of his journey home. He needed to get to a peaceful spot in his mind where he could find some relief, even if that meant staying on topic for hours. He continued:

> On the eighth day, Friday, April 20, we left Lutterberg at 8:15 am. First we walked to Landwerhagen, then Kassel. We spent the night in the next town, Molkershausen. It had been a very good day. We had travelled 40 km.
>
> The next day, day nine of freedom, Saturday, April 21, we left Molkershausen to walk to Gensungen, then on through Filsberg, Lohre, Niedermolbireh, Cappel, Ubermolbirch, Fritslar, and then we slept in Geismaar. Again we were back to our meager 18 km that day.
>
> I felt pretty bad about slowing my friends down. That tenth day, Sunday, April 22, we had to rest the whole day because I, Gustaaf, could travel no more on my bloody stubs of feet. My feet were almost completely broken open. But I had hope in my heart that the next day it would go better for me so that my friends and I could move toward home again.
>
> Except for my ridiculous feet, everything up to this point had gone well. But now all of our food was gone! However we did not yet lose hope or strength

in our conviction to get home. In total, we had travelled 183 km. *Unfortunately,* we still had about 800 km to walk.

So, now and then there would be a bit of an argument amongst us. That happens in every household. And we did think of ourselves as a family. Each argument ended quickly with the simple desire in all of our hearts that tomorrow we would be able to continue our journey—in hope of victory. We were still fighting a war, you see, and victory would be won when each of us entered our childhood homes!

The eleventh day, Monday, April 23, we left Geismaar at 7:00 am. We walked on to Wellen then Wega (Bad-Wildungen), Kundsdorf, Lohlbach, and Dainrode where we stayed the night. 30 km. We had actually made it that far! But now our little group had two men with broken feet. Tomorrow did not look promising. Why was it so difficult for us to get home?

The twelfth day was eventful. On Tuesday, April 24, we left Dainrode at 9:00 am. We were on our way to Frankenberg but we could not get any farther than that one town. Two of us could no longer walk and one of those two was *naturally* me. I felt really down about that.

We saw no other way to go on but to go to the American Military Police, the M.P.s, in Frankenberg, to ask if we could ride along in a car tomorrow.

They took us with them and we got farther again!

Very exciting!

We drove through Bottendorf, Ernthausen, Munshausen, Simthausen, Fordenhausen, Wetter, Niederwetter, Lottingen, Colle, and into Marburg where they let us off and joined us to an army squadron which was attempting to bring order to the chaos of thousands of people like us.

But now we were stuck in Marburg. They gave us a half kilo of bread per day and a quarter kilo of meat each day as well. But the sleeping was very poor in a tent that we had to make ourselves the same night we got there. It was very cold that night. But the cold was the least of our worries.

The worst was the lice ... because of them, we could not sleep. Our clothes were alive! Instead of the sleep we needed so desperately, we talked about our hope of being home soon. But we did not know when we would leave Marburg.

We had gone an extra 10 km on foot plus another 37 km by car that day. Only to be stuck in one place for who knew how long?

Frustrating!

It was the thirteenth day, Wednesday, April 25, and unbelievably, we were held up with the army squadron and in our *tent*!

Maddening!

The fourteenth day was no better. Thursday, April 26, was one of the worst days of our new freedom. At 7:00 pm all the boys, including the six of us, were leaving the military base in Marburg but we found it was with a lot of bad luck. They took us to another, different army camp. Damn! It was 35 hard-earned kilometers back the way we had come!

Sure, the sleeping arrangements were much better with protection from the rain and wind. But, Goddamnit, 35 km farther from home was just...

INSANE!

We had suffered for those kilometers. We had lived that distance as free men and the *Allies* were taking that away from us. It was just unbearable.

I cried.

We *all* cried.

* * *

When I read this portion of my father's memoir, it took me back to that snowy day in my past. I recalled how I thought it was insane to allow men to injure themselves trying to get home only to kill their hope, thoughtlessly, because of a few orders given by men behind desks who knows where?

Reading it for myself, without my parents there, brought more experiences from that afternoon back to me.

Somewhere in the middle of my father's unstoppable story, my mind had stopped trying to comprehend the inner workings of the military efforts in Europe and I must have gazed, unseeing, at my mother.

I do remember, clearly, contemplating how I could have ever hurt these two precious people—the thought still tortured me from time to time. I could not believe I could do such a thing. At times like these—with one so desperate to change the subject and the other unwilling to be diverted from a topic he needed released to the world to save his sanity—I was lost.

I think, I must have mirrored the shell-shocked look on my father's face because my mother began talking as if she could not stop. It made no sense.

"Hey, I think I am going to make new PJs for the boys in fun designs. I will give those to them at Christmas, with love. What do you think?"

I know that I stared past her. I was still lost in my thoughts, not unlike my father. I had hurt them—I had hurt two people that had known enough pain to last two lifetimes.

My father stared into the room as well. He had tears in his eyes. He had found the point in his narration which he had needed to reach. But now, he was not able to let go of the memory which allowed him to hate both sides in the conflict that had ruined his life.

"Don't either of you understand?" he'd shouted. "We were in Neustadt. Practically next door to Halberstadt. They had driven much further than we thought! They had taken us right back to where we had started. We had not realized how far back the truck had taken us while packed in the back like sardines. When we saw where we were, we thought they were taking us back to our prison! Delivering us back to the Nazis!"

"It was horrifying!" he finished breathlessly.

His shouting fell into a dead silence. Our numbed stillness magnified the whistling of the deadly wind outside our home, on that stormy day. I remember feeling buried alive; but I was buried under too much emotion, not snow.

* * *

My dad would not believe that we could not absorb his hate. He wanted us to hate the entirety of both sides of the war, as ludicrous, which it was.

See, my father taught me well. At times, such thoughts escape my mind before I can control them. Ludicrous? Perhaps all war is ridiculous. We are too small to say that and to be heard.

But my mother could not hate her liberators, the Allies.

At times like these there was no release, no balm from my mother's lips.

Hate is a vicious thing, no matter who delivers it. Sometimes there is no escape. So I lived my father's hatred when he spoke, at times like these.

Still my mother had tried. It was babble at this point since no one listened.

"I will make slippers too," she'd continued. "Slippers for everyone! Warm and cozy. We will of course have a Christmas party with your uncle and your cousins. That's always fun. Right, Daddy?"

Silence.

I imagined my father's fork dropping and heard the agonizing swallow again—heartache is a vicious, sometimes rusty, blade.

My mother had rambled on desperately:

"We will bake and cook until the house smells rich and luscious . . . I always thought it was strange that children did not wear slippers here in the winter, or that not all of them wore shoes in the summer . . . strange. Such differences from, from, from home."

"We *are* home, Mama," my father had told her abruptly. "You need to remember and Mary needs to know this story."

Outside, the wind viciously blew ice crystals against our window panes. My dad went on above the sound of the storm:

> We ended up in Neustadt at this new camp. Then on the fifteenth day of our "freedom," Friday, April 27, we tried to get out of the camp and look for a room in town. We finally found a room in the upstairs of a house that was still standing. It was a couple of rooms, actually, where we could organize ourselves once more for the trip home.

We would start again. We lived together in a room in Halberstadt, again, and planned for our freedom, again.

Home looked very far away at this time.

When we left this place, the plan was to be that no one stayed behind and we would be six brave men with only one hope—to get to Belgium as soon as possible.

One thousand miles. On foot. Again.

The recollection of my teenaged "I" and the series of stories my simplemindedness had summoned, had somehow strengthened the gossamer-like connection between my heart and the knowledge of the mental suffering my father had had to endure in his young manhood. The feelings attached to the word *again* make me want to survive all of my challenges with endurance and bravery, and to always try *again*. Those are the very good things my father gave me.

Even though I know it was not really a thousand miles he trudged through to get home, it seemed so to him. He was going home and his message to us was that his journey promised him that very good things would come from his suffering when he did finally, get home. When his storm was over.

* * *

March was still inching spring-ward. Having written my worst episode as a teenager and thereby reliving it, I sat sobbing into fistfuls of tissues in front of my computer screen. I had awoken a guilt which I had thought long buried. I had sharpened the edge of the blade again and relived the hurt my parents had felt because of me.

My husband, when he came in, found me in a soggy jumble of tissues. When I explained what was tormenting me, he threw me a life preserver.

"You were young. Young people deserve forgiveness and the second chances we give them. Your parents loved you and forgave you," he reminded me. "You need to forgive yourself."

I hiccupped.

"You have a great message to give your family. Go ahead and tell it," he urged me softly.

I dried my eyes and held him close to my heart. Then I noticed it had become a perfect late winter day outside. The sun glinted off melting icicles and I inhaled the smell of thawing patches of soil through the slightly open window.

"He was a good man," my husband reminded me.

"Yes, my mother restored him to that." I smiled. "He was the bread and he rose nicely with her leaven."

"She was a good woman, as are you!" He kissed the end of my nose. His green eyes were twinkling in the last hints of a watery, late winter afternoon. And that's when we heard the trill of returning birds! The relaxed feel of recurring spring was certainly in the air. Suddenly my guilt turned to appreciation for what I possessed. I owned a particular knowledge of love that some people only longed for.

I tugged at his wrist and drew him nearer, into the flow of cool, early spring air. His embrace felt like the very arrival of spring. I did indeed have a great message to give!

* * *

I waver now on which details to include in this history. What will make everyone understand what type of people war breeds? What type of people those survivors breed?

I feel this history is so profound and meaningful. But I fear it is so only for me. That it means nothing to the others involved in its living or to those detached and distanced from it, by a lack of experiences.

Did anyone else's parents conquer demons in the night? I believe they did. Many probably still do.

There have been many wars.

Okay. All of the details must be included.

Why have I written down how my parents died? Why am I recording the history of what they left behind? Is this strong desire to retell their story because they also left me behind? Or is it a confessional sort of thing? What must I confess?

I must confess that I feel as though my musings have always answered to the jerking of a puppeteer, my father. I feel like my mother simply carried the scissors to cut the string at times most uncomfortable for her little puppet.

So now that the strings are cut?

I realize that to write their history, *my* history, is to recover my parents from death. It is to allow them to live again. I now know how much I need them to live again. I want them to remain alive inside me.

Writing a family history is to recover oneself, my self.

This work is to discover how I might have been—without the baggage. Sure, no baggage would have been a good thing. I could have been more open, enjoyed more laughter, been more trusting. I could have been free. I would have been more like my mother.

I am more bound to tradition than I would like to be. I am a bit hardened by my father's war and by my own trials in life. Life with the doubts about peoples' character which my father firmly fostered in me, made me suspicious of people who seem too friendly. What are they after? And following orders during my formative years from a man who ran his family like a military machine made me a demanding person. Why is everything not done my way?

Why do I hate people who act entitled—so much?

I do not know the answers to all of this. But I do know that I am a mixture of bread and leaven, waiting to rise. Without the flour, I would be less determined. Without the leaven, I would be terminal OCD.

Okay. Considering where I came from, my parents did their best to make a balanced individual who knows what she wants and who loves, with passion, the life they gave her. I am colourful, like my mother's stories. I try to be open and trusting but I sometimes fall short of making friends. I am too wary, like my father. Then I laugh too loud and attract unwanted attention, like my mother. I fear the opinions of others, like my father.

I am like my parents! A bit of both—as we all are. I can be proud of that.

And although I am shadow-filled, like my father, I am strong beyond his wildest dreams! He gave me convictions.

I have baggage.

So does everyone else. My burden is simply a bit different and it makes me who I am.

* * *

Back in Halberstadt, we came to terms with our anger. We were used to doing that. But our delays made us more determined than ever to get home.

We were no longer prisoners. In fact, the people of Halberstadt had torn down the walls of our former prison and now treated us as guests in their homes. They did not have much but they were happy to share. We realized that they had not been free either when we had first resided in their town. One wrong move and their own countrymen would have turned on them at Hitler's orders.

The food was good. There was 400g of bread per day and two warm meals per day. It was more than double what we got from the Nazis. With the Nazis, the difference was that we always had to work and work and work; then we were forced to work some more. The food provided to us, then, would only come after the work, later, and it would not be half enough for young men who had worked hard all day.

The food was never enough during our captivity. However, getting kicked and punched, you could get plenty of that—as much as you wanted and more. The treatment was typical for the Nazis. They always used brute force and they spread their force throughout all of Halberstadt, not just within our camp.

Even though the Americans forced us back to Halberstadt, we forgave them for they knew not what they did. Is that not what Jesus said? With the Americans, our treatment was completely opposite. It was like Halberstadt had become another place entirely. They always gave us lots of food and we never had to work. Instead of brutality at their hands, the Americans were always ready to have a conversation. And in the evenings, we were free to amuse ourselves. One evening we would go to the cinema and the next we would do something different.

But we were not yet allowed to go home.

Americans hate chaos and apparently they believed that our migration home would be chaos without their help. So far, we did not see it like that and our frustration was growing by the hour.

    Yes. Once upon a time I had steered this man, whose memoir spoke so many times about food, away from his meal.
    It speaks volumes that he forgave me.

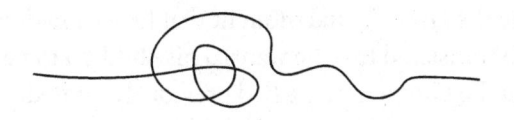

At Odds

The screens along the perimeter of our deck were pulled tight against the cool spring breeze. But the sun, gaining in warmth and light every day, trickled through each tiny aperture like feeble rays of hope.

But it was not hope that I felt while watching it or what I was thinking about this day. I sipped my hot tea and meditated about hardship and all that it could render in the people it touched.

A sparrow darted to and fro across my line of vision, persistently, until I noticed her. Her nest, only partially complete, had blown down during the night. Her hardship had bred determination to succeed in building a new home for the brood she carried inside of her. Her fortitude fit well with my thoughts this morning, but I leaned more toward the spiritual side of things.

I jerked upright in my chair.

"Spirituality!" I gasped. A group of frightened blackbirds at the feeder rose as one, startled by my exclamation and sloshing tea. It was like I had fallen asleep there on the deck, dreaming, to awaken with a clear vision of what to write next. My parents had been at odds over, of all things, God.

Extreme hardship has a way of either perpetuating faith or expurgating spirituality from a person's soul. My father did not realize that his journey home would kill the God he had prayed to while in captivity. His journey transformed him from the inside out. When my father referred to "forgive them for they know not what they do," that was probably the last spiritual thought that he ever had. His God was dead. Which translated to—he wanted his children to believe he was right to deny the God whom he had previously quoted.

So of course, my mother provided the leaven, again, by sending all four of her children to Catholic school. She provided every opportunity for her children to play outdoors in God's creation where we could form our own relationship with God, rather than adopt the blighted connection our father wanted us to have. We played in the snow, rain, sunshine, and she made sure we experienced God's great wilderness! I still own the many pictures she took of her boys in their big, thick snowsuits, pulling sleighs and throwing snow. She told me many years later that she could only whisper to us that God made the snow we loved so much. And only whisper it when our father was not listening. He would have reminded us that the cold gave us the flu or the sniffles, made our clothes wet and uncomfortable, and that God did not have our pleasure in mind when he made it!

I wondered, not for the first time, how could I separate what was atypical to my father, my mother, to my childhood, to our family? Or did I really need to segregate these thoughts, place each aspect alone? All of these unique characteristics had combined to create me. The peculiar melded together inside me. Who was I to separate them? I had no answers.

I watched the sparrow for a bit more. She was happy. Nothing could dampen her spirits; her mind was filled with thoughts of providing for her chicks. That was when I heard my husband's laughter from beyond our pond. It echoed off the water as he chuckled at the antics of our latest Bob who was chasing rabbits in the long grass. Bob's hardship was his size. At 150 pounds, our giant Alaskan Malamute created way too much racket stomping around to ever catch anything. I know that I appreciated his clumsiness more than he did. I did not want him harming the fragile ecosystem that my husband so lovingly tended in our "back forty." My mother had nurtured a love of nature in her children which I did not want disrupted in me by deaths in my own yard . . . as my father had experienced.

That memory reminded me of a childhood trip during which I first realized that my father tended to push not only God, but everyone, away from himself.

When we were young, my mother had helped my brothers convince our father that we should see the Canadian north. So we packed the dog, our cat, and a pot of stew into the car with every other imaginable necessity for wilderness living. We stopped for a bushel of corn on the cob on the way. There were big farm dogs there and our cat did not appreciate them very much. They literally scared the shit out of that cat—all over the pot of stew. Then it raced around the car for a good five minutes before our father stopped laughing long enough to attempt a cleanup! He hated that cat! Yet it was our father who delayed our trip back home from our excursion to fish the cat out from under our cabin in the woods. He would not leave her up there, even if she had ruined our stew. As I said, he was a good man. Not a spiritual one. He "goddamned" that cat and anything else on earth which went against his will. I believe he alienated my brothers that way as well. The boys were strong willed and determined, just like their father. I think we all know how that mixture of testosterone goes.

* * *

My father's diplomatic skills were birthed by rough midwives:

> On the sixteenth day, Saturday, April 28, our day went well but that evening when we went to the cinema . . . the movie had just started. We were five minutes in when everyone started fighting. We fought too, since we had to protect ourselves. Everyone was quite drunk. It started between a group of Russians vs. the French. Within moments, all hell broke loose. Chairs flew over our heads. Then the lights went on and the movie stopped only those few moments into it. With the lights on to identify the culprits, the fighting died down but when they

started the movie again, a repeat of the previous situation took place. The fighting began in earnest this time! Now we all hated one another for ruining the film and our evening. It was crazy. We had no self-control. And this time, some men were using knives.

We saw the weapons and I said, "Come on men, let's get out of here." But just before we hit the door, the Americans came in and put a stop to the conflict by throwing the Russians out. More war. More fighting. More hatred.

There was nothing more! To hell with this!

Another day—gone. Another day without love. Another day without God. I don't think He ever existed. Well at least He did not exist for me anymore. Amen.

It must have been his inner chaos which prevented my father from connecting with his sons. His only way of communicating was through orders and those were not always gracefully received by them. It did come to blows at times and a rift was torn in our family which, to this day, we try to repair with little effect. Still, because our mother believed in God, she never stopped trying to hold her family together. She longed for her grandchildren and her children when they sometimes chose to stay out of the line of fire from our father's hatred for the world. It was a world made impossible for him to accept. He felt that God had made the world to damn him. My mother convinced me that God had made the world so that we could all be happy. I think I believed a mixture of both philosophies. I was a very mixed-up child.

So I became what I find to be a rare bird in our family. A bird that believes in God and that He loves our family such as it is. My father would have scoffed. My mother would have rejoiced, had she witnessed my present relationship with God. Mine is a relationship with my father's God, who does not exist, and my mother's God, who made everything for us. My father's God was the Church, which is an institution I can sometimes not abide, so it is not where my relationship with my God exists. Not *surprisingly*, my God exists in all that He created for us within His love! Thanks to my mother!

My father often wondered aloud if it was God, not Hitler, that had created his suffering for him. That is where my father got stuck. He refused to contemplate God any further. My mother would have said, "Look at what you have now and be happy!" Sincere happiness always eluded my father and I think I know why.

His war was with God.

> The seventeenth day, Sunday, April 29—today, for the first time in twenty-two days, we were able to bathe! You can only imagine what good that did us. One guy thought it was God's will! I told him he was crazy.
>
> "But didn't He stop the war?" the same idiot asked. "I think that was *the Allies*," I told him. I also told him to shut up! He did, especially as on the eighteenth day, Monday, April 30, six men joined us. It was not fun or comfortable with no more room in the barracks for more.
>
> "Surely it will not take much longer before we leave for home," my idiot friend said. I asked him if God had told him that.
>
> The next day left nothing special to report. God remains absent from our situation.

My father's transformation from innocent boy to cynical anti-spiritualist occurred over five years. The years of WWII. The effects lasted his entire remaining days. My mother's care never cured him of his Godlessness, and he continued to sleep through Sunday service, and to apologize all of the way home, as long as I can remember. When her children were grown, my mother stopped trying and stopped dragging him to church. He said he liked it better that way.

His simmering hatred of anything or anyone spiritual sustained him for four years after my mother's death. During that time, he liked to turn that hatred upon his caregivers, and I felt his wrath. Now I know why my brothers avoided that onslaught. Many times, I felt I should leave him to his own devices. Still, I am glad that I did not abandon him and that his passing was a gentle thing. He knew my mother waited for him at the gates. I pray he made it. I know he did. God loved him.

***

I find myself back on the deck now, later in the day. The sparrow's nest is finished and ready for her family. My husband is here in the wicker loveseat beside me and the sounds of the trickling waterfall in the pond are like a million raindrops strumming against a window. God's world is a great creation at moments like this.

Rudy had his coffee and I sipped tea from my favourite rambling rose cup. Our quiet discussion centred on how I had come to possess such an oddly pious idea of anti-dogma regarding the Church. While I devoutly respect the word of God, I rebel against the idea that Church doctrine forces believers to rigidly adhere to specific styles and modes of worship. Does it matter if I pray using my own words or with those the Church wants me to use? I find dogmatic prayer and chants confining and unrealistic. My conversations with God are heartfelt and sincere in my own words. I want my prayers to sound like they come from me when He hears them! I do not wish to repeat rehearsed prayers that are rendered meaningless by memorization.

My father hated dogmatic restrictions. My mother worshipped as though the world was created for her. I hear them both in my explanations of my spiritual quirks.

It took all evening for me to relate these terms of my peculiar slant on earthly commitment to God, to my conventionally faithful husband. The war of division in my heart between dogma and individual devotion left me feeling chilled to the bone. So my husband's solid presence felt like a warm quilt around me. His caress was a balm to my inner turmoil.

"You are a good person, Mary," he told me.

I fell asleep trying to believe those words, next to my rock, my quilt—my saviour.

And I dreamt of my parents in the presence of God. I saw them at a great table. Both of them were smiling.

My father's mouth had been overfull.

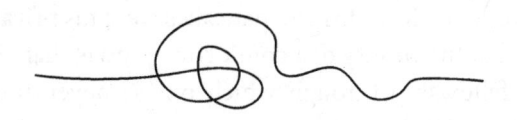

God Has a Name

Reading books, of any kind, can be a sanctuary. For days after that quiet evening of coming to terms with my conflicting ideas about faith, I read. I read a whole series of mystery books about a small, lost village that no one could find but where anyone could feel at home. It seemed a magical place that I wanted to find. I wanted to live there. I wanted to be at peace with my thoughts. However, that was not meant to be. My mind always dwelt upon my father's Godlessness; on the fact that he had been so alone without the confidante I so often turn to in times of trial. Who did my father turn to in the darkest hours of his endless night? Whose voice did he hear when my mother slept?

Was it the voice of a saviour?

Or was it the scream of a tormentor?

I prayed that some form of solace had survived his war.

> The twentieth day, Wednesday, May 2, was the day we received twenty cigarettes. It was the first time we had seen cigarettes since leaving Halberstaat the first time. And on the twenty-first day, *pancakes*! We made pancakes! So naturally, we all ate very well.

The secret is out. This is why my father always begged my mother to make pancakes! His first good meal, after years of captivity, was pancakes.

I now wonder if cigarettes and pancakes were his private succor.

I believe that the beauty of a comforting God is that His presence generates a fellowship through which one is never alone. But my father was alone. His love of food and cigarettes were what he walked away with from the war. He swore he would never be hungry or deprived again. From his memoirs, the focus on food tells the story of his new religion.

> From now on, we receive 500g of bread per day! The difference between getting a lot less and then, here, much more is outstanding. We now realize that when the Nazis said, "Where the Americans are, there is hunger," was not true. We have witnessed the opposite. We have experienced full bellies for the first time in a long while. The Allies saved us with food. It was not God!

Spirituality through food—surely my father is not the first or the only person to fall into that pit. His memoirs focused on food at many intervals, and I cannot say that I blamed him. His written memories also serve to show that sometimes the worst of war was not always the fighting but the boredom. Soldiers must always wait. Wait for orders, wait for chow, wait for something to happen—my father made light of the waiting. So many times I read, "Today, nothing special to announce . . ." Then, finally, something happened:

> It was our twenty-third day trying to get home. It was Saturday, May 5, when we heard that Holland, Denmark, and more of NW Germany had been liberated! What news! Surely something would now be done about our situation!! Our war was over for good! We would be going home to our families! We cried! And then we cried some more!

Reading this section of the memoir, I could feel the jubilation and I experienced the choking tears. I realized that until then, my father had not truly believed that he was free. He had still felt like a prisoner—dependent upon the military machine surrounding him for his lifeblood. My father had still felt like a captive animal waiting for its next cue to move. The realization left me feeling immensely troubled. No wonder he never recovered. No wonder he had horrible nightmares. *No wonder he was angry.*

The next entry was plain—and shocking.

> The twenty-fourth day, Sunday, May 6, *nothing special to report.* Then on Monday they told us that Germany had surrendered. But we did not know if it was true. Why did they torment us like this?

How were men, so obviously broken, supposed to react to such mixed signals?
Peace.
No. Not yet.
Freedom.
No. Go back.
An end to suffering.
No, you cannot go home yet.
Just this anguish alone would have set me screaming! It was no different than being held in a prison camp. No wonder they could not believe their ears or their hopes. Their lives had become a prison of despair. Their hope had become focused on bread and pancakes.
Frustrating. Maddening. Insane.
Many soldiers never recover from such treatment. The soldier my father had been—never recovered. It was too late for him.

> Tuesday, May 8, the twenty-sixth day. Today—the BIG NEWS! Germany has completely laid down their weapons! There is PEACE!

Dare we hope?

I sat, in the midst of my scattered books, wishing that I could find refuge in them again but I kept coming back to somber thoughts of my father's total absence of hope. He should have been able to rejoice.

The war was over!

But it was not finished for my father and his friends. As the world breathed its relief, they cringed in hopelessness.

The hollowness they must have felt crept between me and my books. Silence seemed to swallow me and threatened to steal my every thought before it was born. I heard the doleful hoot of an owl from outside the open window; it echoed in my soul like a reflection of bleakness. Then a breeze rustled some papers I had recently thought were filled with profound thought.

How profound can anything I write be if I have never truly experienced total disillusionment?

Is my empathy for my father born not of understanding but of something as simple as pity?

Is it only pity?

Perhaps at times it was.

No. I loved him, deeply.

I admired his strength. Who goes on, doggedly, when they have lost all hope?

Godless survivors do!

My father did.

What we shared was a communion!

Again, the cool, spring breeze whooshed in through the window. Again, it rustled the papers and the very pages of the novel I held. It was time to visit with my father *again*.

* * *

There was another road trip with my father that blessed us with the discovery of our mutual understanding. At the time, I was about eleven years old and my father was in business for himself. He had opened a flooring store. I had accompanied him on a trip to Hamilton, Ontario, to pick up an order of floor tile to finish a big job he had landed.

Usually, on these trips, we stopped at a restaurant named Gulliver's Travels where they served the most delightful Boston cream pie, north of Boston! He always ordered us both a huge slice, with coffee for him and milk for me. This time was no different, but we took the items to go. He drove further and parked near the entrance to Hamilton's famous Royal Botanical Gardens.

We ate our treats in a remote corner of the garden, sitting on a log with a gurgling stream trickling over our bare feet. He told me that this shady place, with the sun breaking through the canopy above us, was *freedom*. He said the pie was like food from my mother's fairy-tale heaven. Then he shoved a big spoonful of pie into his mouth and sighed.

I looked at him, then leaned back and stared at the sky-high tree-tops above us seemingly reaching toward the light. And I remember clearly thinking that this moment was communion for us. We experienced extraordinary fellowship for that half hour of heaven.

After that day, I believed that my father knew *his* God personally.

I still believe he had a relationship with a personal God, to this very day, because that is what he had told me in his own private way. His God was not El Shaddai, El Elyon, Adonai, Yahweh, Jehovah, El Olam, Elohim, Qanna, or even Jesus.

His God celebrated solitude and food and He was named *Freedom*.

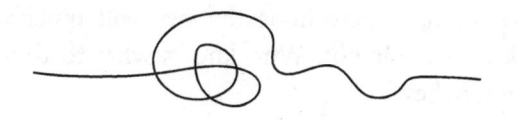

A Fine Day

One would think that, after having survived a world war, those still living would have found some precious serenity in their hard-won lives. And that their homecomings would be serene and comforting. Yet it was only the world outside of where all the action had taken place that returned to peace.

Serenity, true tranquility, could not withstand the onslaught of insecurity and determined new resolutions invading minds surrendering to PTSD. My father confessed that his survival mantra became one of singular determination. He never wanted anyone, himself included, to experience hurt ever again. He realized through constant repetition of this thought that if that were to happen, if misery again entered his life through any small chinks in his armour, it would utterly devour him.

At the end of WWII, it is true that happiness was, once more, an option for the former soldiers released into a new world. But my father and his friends felt that they had no choices left to them as the instruments of allied law and order rolled over them.

PEACE?

Perhaps some of them faked a restless peace on the outside. But, for my father, there was no peace within. Not really.

Now we have new hope that we will quickly be back home! Or not. Who knows what to think? I cannot believe.

Still, on Wednesday, May 9, the twenty-seventh day of our freedom, now that the war is over if we dare to hope, it is good weather too! A nice day for all.

There is still one major thing that bothers us—how do we get home to Belgium? Is everyone we love still alive?

Everyone still alive? Peace? Not in a Godless universe—not within the haze of PTSD which is where my father resided. Frustration and waiting, most of all wanting, lived in his soul now.

Whether or not everyone was still alive at home, that is the big question. Dare we hope for the best? We are waiting with great anticipation for our orders to go home to Belgium. Great anticipation!

Free men—waiting for orders to return home. Is our home not where all of us would run to if freed from hostile confinement? Would we wait in "great anticipation" or just run? Orders to go home? Would we truly need them? Yet my father and his friends waited, as they had waited while caged. Still caged in their minds, they could not summon a new decision to begin a second journey home. That joy had been robbed from them when the allies tried to help them and had returned them to the scene of the crime. Halberstadt. Hell!

The twenty-eighth day, Thursday, May 9. Nothing to announce and with a lot more days like this to come, hope escapes me. Now we wait impatiently for the big news that we can pack everything, to leave in the morning, to go back to Belgium. Home. Many more days . . . just waiting and waiting and waiting.

It seems unbelievable, to those who have never been imprisoned, that these men just did not pack up and go home. The waiting must have been horrendous! The not knowing the fates of their loved ones must have eaten at their souls. And the souls which had not survived the war were the first to be devoured by waiting time. My father traveled beyond the point of recovery while he waited. A man who learned to hate so thoroughly must have cherished his family deeply before the demise of his ability to love. His hatred of all things military, confining, and non-progressive became something that he tasted daily with his bread and pancakes. Orders, imprisonment, and stagnation produced a shell of the young man who had loved his mother, father, and five sisters more than life itself. The shell was only filled once again when he found my mother.

"She is the one I will marry!" he announced from across the room.

But that is another part of this history entirely.

Many more days . . .

> Then the following day, June 1, at 9:30 am, we packed up and left for Newstadt! We felt like our breath was clean and fresh. All at once we could breathe again and it was good! We left in cars headed for Mecklenbeek. In cars! Then in Mecklenbeek, we were allowed to board *trains* and all the while we were always getting closer and closer to Belgium! *Surely* there would be no more setbacks. We were being taken home! We even dared to hope that this was true! The cars drove on and on and did not stop! I remember thinking that, "*IF* all goes well, we could get home to see everyone again after this long time."
>
> We drove through the night. We drove through small town after small town for what seemed like days. We

only stopped for fuel where we could find it. Then we drove on and on. Small town after small town until all became a huge blur. We drove a route from Bosenhilsen to Talenberg! I had no time to figure out distances now. We were getting close to the border!

In very early June, I had lost track of the date—but it was at 10:30 am—we crossed the border from Germany into Holland! Into freedom! Into LIFE!

To say that we crossed the Dutch border with relieved hearts is to grossly insult our level of excitement! There are no words. No words can relate such joy, excitement, and relief. We were alive, free, and almost home.

We were getting very close to Belgium. We prayed that the train would not stop!

We had entered Holland at Heerlem. The train was not as fast as before the war with many repairs to the tracks and to the train. It traveled at a snail's crawl!

Then *finally*, after three days and three nights more, we rolled into Belgium. No border could stop us now!

Dates do not matter to me as I write this but it was 2:30 pm, on a fine day, when we reached Luik! We were in Belgium, albeit in the French district, opposite to where we lived.

The mix up in dates, times, and city names at this point in the memoirs can be attributed to my father's excitement. But the main message was abundantly clear: They were home!

They were in a Belgian city, Luik. The name must have sounded like the chimes in heaven.
But, to my father, it was still not home; and there was no heaven.

> Luik. There we were forced to stay for two days. Two days before we were free to leave. No one knew why. Everyone protested. Everyone cried. I believe I sobbed...
>
> After two weary days, we were finally allowed to go home by car or by train, whichever we chose. That was the first choice I had made for myself in a very long time. It felt, tasted, and reeked of freedom! I drank in that feeling as I made my request.
>
> FINALLY, still in early June, 1945, I arrived home after my long and weary absence. I was weary of war. Weary of life. Worn out.
>
> Now we are free of those Nazi bastards!

These were the final lines in my father's memoirs. The memoirs which I had asked him to pen. They did not tell the whole story of my father's ordeal. It made me cry to think that I had had a hand in bringing all of his horrible memories to the fore. They were memories which may have benefited him more if they had stayed in hiding. But they were memories which aided me in understanding the man who gave me the life he found at the end of a very long road, in Luik.
No. There was no tranquility in my father's world.
He never found it, even with my mother to help him.
PTSD is like that.
It takes hold and never lets go.
It leaves one seeking solitude and freedom.

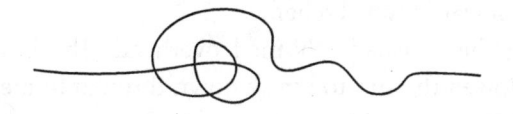

Emotional Deadness

I watched the sun sparkle on the tops of tiny wavelets in the canal. I was standing at a crossroads of sorts. It is where the canal meets the river in our town and the engineers had built an aqueduct, beneath the canal, to allow the river to continue to flow. I watched the water flow by slowly. I hoped a big ocean tanker would come by as they had when I had watched the water with my father those many years ago. But there was no boat right now, not even on the horizon. It was a slow day on the water. All was quiet on the canal front.

Not so on the river's shores! Bank beaver lived there and were busy babbling in the warm sun. The sounds of their grunts and squeaks were joyous as their kits played in the sunshine on the low slopes beside the river. I just stood there and breathed in both the summer heat and the sounds of the rhythmic lapping water. It was glorious!

Long walks with my dogs had always been a comfort for me when I could not cope. Writing out my father's memories had caused me to take more and more walks. I would be working diligently—then suddenly up and go for a stroll. Today I unexpectedly found myself near the canal in a wilderness area with Bob sniffling around in the brush. Bob is after the bank beavers. I am after an escape from sharing my father's distress. I am my father's daughter. I inherited his need for solitary moments of introspection when any form of misery overwhelms me. So here I stand, with an ancient canopy above my head to create a protection from the hot summer sun.

I walked onward toward relief.

Suddenly the sunshade thinned overhead. The beaver-chewed trees had allowed the sun to streak down through to me. It was like the finger of God, and it hit me right in the face.

Nothing was changed. I still felt troubled.

But, for a brief instant, something was changed in that flash of brilliance. I could almost feel my burden getting lighter.

Sunshine can do that for Canadians who suffer from a lack of bright rays for almost half of each year! I looked back at the dazzling sunlight illuminating the many burrows where the bank beavers nested and where they now hid from my snooping dog. Their situation made me quickly realize that my discomfort had merely retreated into its lair for a passing moment.

As my sight turned inward, my brilliant day vanished as though clouds had rolled in unexpectedly, darkening my vision. The beavers' retreat into their burrows when Bob came too close to them made me remember how often my father retreated into emotional deadness when experiences came too near to his memories and caused him pain.

* * *

I remember being seventeen and watching my father bury himself in a mountain of numbness to survive my mother's illness. It was a time when my father's darkness affected me greatly and left broad scars on my adytum.

I had studied for one of my college exams long into the night. I was determined to ace this one! The fact that my mother had gone to a doctor's appointment the day before was lost on my super-focused brain.

My parents' announcement that my mother needed to reduce her stress was not lost on me but it was tucked away behind some more important facts needed for the all-consuming exam. I do remember mumbling something about her staying in bed for a few days until her new medicine took control of her soaring blood pressure.

Then I went on with my studying. Scar number one.

The next morning, I awoke to the sounds of pacing—and cursing. When I saw my father's face, I knew he was battling emotions he could not endure.

And—my mother was gone.

He had taken her to the hospital in the dead of night. She had been beside herself with pain. She had told him that her head was exploding. Their departure had been a whisper; she had not wanted to disturb me from my rest.

I had slept through her ordeal. Scar number two.

As my father told me this, I saw his mood snap from panic to desperation. I could hear that he was planning for her to survive this brain hemorrhage by sheer will—on his part.

He was suffering.

And, when my father suffered, I knew I would make myself endure anything to have his dream come true. I would save him a touch less heartache through pain of my own.

"You have an exam today?" He barked out the question.

"Yes. But..."

"Go to it. I am going to the hospital. They are taking her to Hamilton General this morning."

"But I can..."

"Go! And don't you dare fail!"

"I can't..."

"What?" He practically screamed.

He was angry now. All signs of hurt were wiped clear off his brow and were replaced by an indescribable fixation—a granite face that demanded that all would remain normal until my mother returned home.

"You will write that exam and the others after it! And you will pass every one! Do you hear me?"

"But..."

"You heard me, Mary!" he shouted. "I will take care of your mother! Don't you dare let us down." He ended in a softer voice.

My emotions, along with his own, were dismissed. My mind leaked the studied facts incessantly as I watched him leave. My mother lay on what might be her deathbed and I went to write insignificant facts for the sole purpose of keeping my father sane.

Scar number three.

I barely passed my exams and my father barely made it.

My mother survived.

I studied at her bedside and struggled with extreme guilt. I wanted to be with her at all times. My father would not have it. That was his place.

And I had my place. I had been told. Scar number four.

The fact that my father separated me from them at this crucial time tore my heart out. Exams can be deferred. My mother's health could not. My father and I argued *every day*. His resolve never wavered, and I had been trained, from birth, never to disappoint him for fear of loosing the dragon of his temper.

In the end, it was a luckless nurse who awoke that beast. I had just entered my mother's hallway with my stack of books when I heard my father yelling at the top of his lungs, his voice cracking with anger.

"She was alone with that crazy woman! You put that creature in here while my wife lay helpless and afraid! I should kill you now! Where is that doctor? I'll kill him too! With my bare hands ... don't think I don't know how!"

I got to the room as he lunged over my sedated mother toward the hapless nurse.

"Dad! Stop! What's going on?"

"They aren't caring for her! They almost got her killed, putting some huge German assassin in here with her! I ... "

"Assassin? Dad please! *Stop!*" I pleaded. He looked me right in the eye and spat on the floor by the nurse's feet.

"Dad, calm! You have to take care of Mom!"

"What do you think I am trying to do? I ... "

"Sit! I won't let Mom wake up to this! DO YOU UNDERSTAND?" I annunciated forcefully. "She needs calm!"

My father looked at my mother's peaceful face and stroked her hair, once, before he fell into a chair. "Tell her what you did, you bitch!" he shouted to the nurse before he took my mother's hand and began to sob.

It was only then that I noticed my mother's twin room held only her bed. I turned to the nurse and we stepped into the hallway.

As it turned out, Vilma Schmidt had had brain surgery two weeks previous to her joining my mother in the double room after leaving ICU. She had been in and out of consciousness all that day. Her brain was still trying to heal and she was sometimes bewildered and lost.

My mother had undergone a spinal tap just that morning and was confined to her bed—strapped in to restrict her movement.

Vilma was a big, strong woman. She had awoken while my father was out on a coffee run. She had lumbered over to my mother's bed and leaned in to get a confused look at the petite creature strapped to the other bed. My mother had awoken and screamed while she rang the emergency bell frantically.

The grotesque bruising on Vilma's face would have frightened anyone. But in my mother's case, who recognized the strong German heritage which also marked her face, it was terrifying.

My father, as he exited the elevator, had heard the screams and the flow of Belgian words interspersed with calls for help. Coffee flew to the floor and the unfortunate nurse arrived at the room just in time to tackle my father's wrath. Vilma only escaped being physically assaulted by my father by the nurse's arms around his middle. Help arrived and Vilma was wheeled out quickly, strapped to her bed, and placed in "solitary."

This was the day that I realized that my father was not the only PTSD casualty in our family. Hypervigilance had lived inside my mother, quite comfortably, until circumstances awoke the horror of growing up during the Nazi occupation of her homeland.

Scar number five.

Yes. I remember being seventeen and suffering the horrors of war in a hospital room, in Hamilton, Ontario. I remember transitioning from young girl to aged soul through one conversation with a nurse while listening to my father cry. Then he refused to be diverted from his sadness for weeks, even after my mother returned home.

And I learned that when anyone is sad for too long, everyone around them becomes miserable.

* * *

I blinked. Miraculously, the sun was still shining; Bob, the birds, and the bank beavers were still at happy odds. Bob flushed a wild turkey just then and as it sprang up and fluttered against a tree trunk trying to flee; the day returned to summer from the dreary grey of a winter hospital room.

Suddenly, the pleasant day was returned to me but I felt my scars—even in the light.

* * *

I meet new people almost every day. I greet them cordially yet sense my barriers going up. Will they hurt me? It is like meeting people with both arms stretched out in front of my heart to ward them off. Stay away! Don't hurt me.

I learned well from two parents with PTSD. Doctors have now labeled the symptoms of PTSD.

Hypervigilance. Check.

Mood swings. Check.

Emotional numbing. Check.

Irritability. Check.

Can one inherit PTSD? Check.

This list of diagnoses hangs between me and the world.

These words will never drift away.

Scars numbered six, seven, eight, nine, and ten.

* * *

I inhaled the scents of summer deeply and called to Bob. The peaceful day tried to soothe me but I was staring into myself, absorbed by the introspection I had sought. I worried that my ability to seek within myself would be my ruination. I remember too much, too vividly.

I worried thus, as the sun glared down at me and shouted *life*! But I closed my eyes to the sun as I got Bob into the car. My tears trickled out at the corners like drops of realization.

My parents had been genuinely troubled people.

Just as I am.

* * *

At the end of WWI, a man named Pierre van Paassen wrote his take on that war. He wrote:

> A boy, who was a piano teacher in civil life, taught me how to twist a long butcher knife, which was fastened to the end of my rifle, into the soft part of an adversary's body, while a gentleman who once sold postage stamps introduced me to the gentle art of crawling up stealthily behind an enemy sentinel and strangling him to death with bare hands before he could give the alarm. Little by little we learned the whole modern technique of serial murder. In less than three months, we were deemed sufficiently expert in assassination, theft, and arson to be sent over to France...[2]

Later on in the book, he wrote:

> That war is a crime, futile, loathsome, and all the rest of it, is universally recognized today... Why is it

---

[2] Pierre van Paassen, *Days of Our Years* (N.Y., New York: Hillman-Curl, Inc., 1939), 66.

that, far from having been abolished, a new and more frightful kind of warfare than any that has ever been waged in the past, seems to be facing humanity."[3]

Paassen sensed the impending doom of WWII as though he also sensed the trembling hearts of many more expert assassins, thieves, and arsonists. This time they would be armed with mechanical weapons to enhance their effectiveness.

He described my father's war as a kind of warfare more frightful than any that had come before it. He was correct in his assumption. The mechanical demolition of Europe and the assassination of millions upon millions of men and women, left my father and other survivors of WWII with inner visions that were never mouthed or even hinted at. These heroes instinctively knew that what they held inside their minds was something too horrific even to attempt to cleanse from their psyche. My father would never think to include how he was trained or what he was forced to commit in order to survive—other than to tell us he was forced to ride a horse, which he had always feared.

How can any essentially good person, who through no real fault of his own and who now considers himself an assassin, be expected to love and live life with the same passion he had lived with before five long years of hatred?

My father could not.

He simply hated.

Many good men befriended hatred after that war. Determined to forget their nightmares, all of them, including my father, were in a stampede to erase every trace of their shame and humiliation at what they had done to survive. The war had performed an incisionless lobotomy on these men which left them restless in spirit and which bred in them inexpressible contempt. Little did they know that everyday life was to be a monotony for them. Their restlessness would never allow them to be joyous as they wished to be. Their

---

[3] Ibid. 68.

contempt for anything to do with the war would be magnified by friends and relatives starved to hear all that had happened to them. They did not yet realize that they would not understand the people they had left behind at the beginning of the war. The soldiers who had left were changed beings; but so were the people that they had loved. *Something* had grown between them.

Just like a distance had grown between the men of war themselves.

It took a few readings of the memoirs to figure out one very important detail.

Once in Luik, my father and his five "best friends" parted ways to go to their respective family homes. What they all found at home was not written. The detail which could easily have been missed was that they were not *really* best friends. Once they parted in Luik, they never saw one another again. The men my father had traveled with were a ragtag group of displaced boys whom the Nazis had forced together as a work crew. My father had grown into manhood along with the other five during their imprisonment in Germany. They were from six different parts of Belgium. They had been united only by the fact that they spoke the same language and had all been held captive in the same hell hole.

It was no shock to me to realize how close my father had felt to the comrades he had grown to love while they were forced to work side by side. It was surprising to understand why he broke all ties with them once they entered their homeland. My father cut his ties with all things and everyone that reminded him of his ordeal. It was part of his destructive self-preservation practice to ignore that his suffering had ever happened. But his nightmares would not let him forget his anguish at having witnessed innumerable crimes of serial murder. He had seen murders every day in the camps, murders which had occurred much too easily in the hell where he had lived for five long years. His vision of the world had become tarnished with memories of a series of violent incidents which history has unfortunately seen repeated since the beginning of time.

* * *

My father had been lucky. He had found his family intact! His parents had welcomed him home with sobbing tears of joy. And his five sisters fussed and caressed him until he hugged them back.

There was the crux.

His family found it first. He needed to be coaxed into hugging the people who loved him. Something was indeed broken. His adytum was lifeless, with his mind stuck in a vicious cycle of PTSD. Post traumatic stress disorder had not yet been defined by the medical profession, in 1945. My father's symptoms were ignored as something that would go away with time.

He married my mother before that time was up.

He had children before that time was up.

My mother tried to heal him with no knowledge of what was wrong.

His children loved him with no understanding of what was wrong.

That time was never up, as long as he lived.

It is a testament to the strength of the man who I call my father that he lived his life to the fullest of his ability after the war. His was a strength that grasped manically at the life he wanted while he was tormented daily by memories that no one should be called upon to endure. The deaths he had witnessed were haunting in themselves, but the starvation and horrible deprivations he had borne lived on inside him.

* * *

It is my belief that God dwells within us as an integral part of our very being. Inside each human being is a place where God exists. That is my adytum.

I also believe that the horrible symptoms of PTSD lived inside my father where his soul had used to dwell. If God indeed dwells within us, then I know with no uncertainty that my father was lost.

He was lost. And he was alone. He was without God. He could no longer bring his soul back to life. He experienced his existence without inner meaning.

Such a life can only lead to conflict.

Such a life can only lead to struggle.

Such a life is a shame when all a person with PTSD needs is a way to find peace. But such a life left my father hearing the shrieking of crows over Flanders, while others heard the larks of freedom sing.

My father lived with rage and in dread, without the Triune God he had loved as a child. His soul missed the creator, the nurturer, and the sustainer. His heart was only a lonely part of its former self but he tried to share it openly and willingly as best he could.

While he could fake his wholeness for the most part, his emptiness left him unfulfilled and searching for a pathway toward peace. It was a pathway that led him across the world to a new life and to new beginnings for everyone who loved him.

* * *

My pastor, the Reverend Jim, once wrote, "A person without God is like a feather in a perpetual wind, blown all over the place without any control or choice in where to rest."

As his country tried to rebuild itself, my father tried to recreate his life. He had been a very young cigarmaker before the war. The factory where he had begun his career had been demolished during an Allied bombing raid designed to clear out the Nazi troops which had occupied his hometown. The only profession known to him was gone.

He could have continued his father's business of thatching roofs, but no one was interested in straw roofs anymore. They wanted something more solid and comforting after the devastation they had witnessed.

And my father could not breathe freely—as he once had.

The love of his family and their sheer joy at having recovered their son and brother was not enough to nurture him back to health. His future seemed, to him, a desolate place, in a country that had allowed her boys to be taken by the Nazis without a fight.

He was too angry.

Too hurt.

Too mistrustful.

Too suspicious.

He quickly decided that he would marry the woman he had fallen in love with. He felt that she was the one who could sustain him. He believed that he could carry on with her by his side. He swore he would become the creator, nurturer, and the sustainer of his own family.

And he swore he would do a better job than God had done for him!

There was a glitch. Her father had died shortly after the war. Her mother thought it was too soon after his death for her daughter to marry. But, as a young woman who had endured and survived a war, she was ready to defy her mother and prove that she could heal her new love. They married and tried to begin their lives together as though misfortune was a thing only of their past.

They immediately gave birth to a son. My father had already realized that the roofing business was going under and that his little family was not prospering in this country. Not in Belgium. Not in a place that had suffered severely during a war he wanted to, no, *needed* to forget. He believed that his nightmares would stop without the reminders of WWII all around him.

They would emigrate! They would say goodbye to this place which held only bad memories and the families of their youth. Canada began calling my father's name. He had heard his wife tell the stories of how the Canadians freed Belgium's cities one by one. Canada would surely be the place which could create, nurture, and sustain a new and happy life for them!

They left Belgium shortly after his decision was made. No amount of their families' coaxing could contain them. Two of my father's sisters and their young families went with them to the new world.

Going to America, to Canada, became a catchphrase in many households throughout Europe. The influx of new immigrants into Canada became a way for Canada to survive the massive losses of manpower they had suffered through two world wars. Moncton, New Brunswick, would be their first Canadian experience—but was that far enough from his torment to still my father's demons?

***

They left Belgium in a rush to liberty. It was a rush not unlike the brave charge my father had experienced on his way home from Germany. They sought liberty from the misery which was still foremost in his mind. They left with next to nothing in their possession but with desperate hope in their hearts.

And—they left with twin boys in my mother's belly.

The sea journey was an experience which left my mother hating boats, and anything to do with water, for the rest of her life. Ill and cold, they reached the Canadian coast and boarded a train for Moncton. It was the start of a very long winter.

There was a family of Dutch immigrants in Moncton who volunteered to billet new arrivals to Canada; they housed those who had nowhere else to go as yet. It was a great kindness which they extended freely to my parents and their baby son. My parents were allowed to recover from their long journey and to make arrangements for the next leg of their trip into Ontario. They remained in Moncton for only a few short weeks. Then they made their way to Elmwood, Ontario.

They traveled to Elmwood by train, which took some time. They had had no idea how far apart locations in Canada could be. It surprised them to see how slowly trains traveled in the winter, in Canada, in 1952.

The home they had arranged to rent turned out to be a rather threadbare establishment. The wind blew freely through ill-kept windows and eaves which had not been repaired in years. My mother was known to say that she thought the wind would carry them all away into the night while they slept or froze to death. She likened that house to an igloo and swore she would never move further north into less "settled" regions of Canada.

Elmwood, however, she always remembered fondly for its friendly Canadian neighbourliness. They had been in that small town for less than a day when neighbours began to arrive, one after the other, with loads of firewood. Soon the old house was toasty warm if still a bit drafty. They received enough wood to warm their little home for the entire winter. The kindness of strangers, my mother would say, saved the lives of her newborn twin babies. Their new friends delivered blankets and food and baby clothes for their town's newest citizens. The heartfelt gifts warmed my mother from the inside out. They lived and socialized with their new friends while they tried to learn how to be Canadian. My mother always said they had learned from the best!

Still, these were baffling times. One summer, the kindly neighbours delivered a bushel of corn to their door. They thanked their friends profusely; then they stared blankly at the sack of corn when the kindly friends had left. They believed that their neighbours thought they were going to raise cattle or chickens in their yard. Corn was what one fed to livestock in Belgium. They quietly buried the generous gift of corn in their backyard and shook their heads. Shortly after, they were invited to a corn roast where they learned that corn was not meant solely for animals in Canada. They loved *sweet* corn. They never buried another cob in their lives!

The best gift they received from the good people of Elmwood was a lifesaver. Men in town had found a job for my father and the husbands of his sisters. The logging company nearby had been short staffed since the war. They were willing to take on these three new men. My father's sisters had married big, strong men. My father was a small man but he willingly became "the smallest logger." While the others sawed and cut the wood, my father was assigned to the truck. He would haul the wood. He never tired of telling the story of no roads in the woods, dirt roads out of the forest, no door or brakes on the truck, and his lack of a license to drive! But he took the job and did his best! They stayed in Elmwood until the mill shut down due to the owner's death but not before they had learned a lot about the industry involved with Canadian lumber.

***

There is a darker side to my parents' lives in Elmwood, my father's side: a side told by a lost soul.

When the kindly neighbours brought firewood and essentials for his newborn babies and young son, my father could not stem his mistrust and suspicions. What did these people want in return? What would he be required to do for them? Did they think he could not provide for his family? These questions always coloured my father's recollection of those times. The kindliness of strangers made him nervous when so much had been expected of him, and so much had been taken away from him, in his "previous" life.

And the work! Although he was willing to work hard for his family, it was still very hard work for a slight man who used to roll cigars and fiddle with airplane parts. And it was work that he felt resembled his captivity in Germany too closely. Being driven into the woods in the early morning was like being driven into the labour sites in Halberstadt. He could not separate the two in his PTSD-driven mind. Although coming home to a loving wife and his children was quite different from returning to the prison camp at night, the poor home they rented and its drafty winter made him unable to forget the cold of a German winter without a coat. The memories, the nightmares which would not let him rest, created for him a drudgery which took him back in time and kept him from being truly happy with his life.

The man my father had become loved his family dearly. The Godlessness of his soul brought him struggle and conflict which at times seemed self-created. The inconsistencies in his personality would at times frighten the family he loved so much.

In the surrounding areas near Elmwood were many small communities of German and Dutch Mennonites. While the people of Elmwood did everything in their power to make my father and his family feel welcome and secure in their town, my father never failed to notice that these Mennonite people kept themselves aloof from the town. He saw it as a slight toward himself and his family. He did not consider that it was their religious choices which kept them separate from others. He was angry with them for being German. He ignored the fact that most of them were Dutch. He was suspicious of these "cults" as he called them. He said that all they needed to turn was a new Hitler—

He was afraid.

No. He was terrified.

And my mother was sad. She missed her life in her hometown, with her busy social life there which had included many relatives and lifelong friends. My father was also sad. He missed his family in Belgium as well, but he reminded our mother that their love for their children and their plans for their futures meant more than their own hardships.

My father *again* made a decision. Since most of the lumber cut near Elmwood was shipped to the Niagara Region where construction was booming, they would relocate to Southern Ontario. He told her the population was thicker there and that there was better shopping and housing and schools. He told her he was sure he could find a job there too. But with three young children in tow, my mother once again asserted her independence for their sake. She told my father that he should go down to the Niagara Region first and find a job. When he had found the job and a house, he could come get them. She was lividly unwilling to part from the new friends who had helped them so much. And she disagreed that the Mennonites were *out to get them*. Still, she understood her husband's dread. He was surrounded by German family names, German street names, German business names—by everything German. He did not differentiate between German and Nazi or between German and Dutch Mennonites. All represented a real threat to him, to his family.

His struggle with PTSD raged on.

And the move took place.

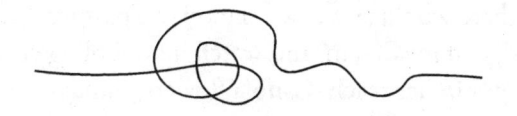

The Farm . . .

A few days later, I was thinking about my parents' move into the Niagara Region as I drove home from my daughter's house on the eastern shore of Lake Huron. It was a long drive which provided me with the opportunity to think after the hustle and bustle created by two rambunctious grandsons. Oli and Abe never stopped until they slept. My days spent with Laura and her family were never uneventful.

The quiet afforded by the long drive home was a blessing which fostered thought, while the farm country of Southern Ontario, rolling by on either side of this speeding room, always made me long for life on a farm—as I imagined it. For this drive time at least, life slowed and allowed my daydreams to come alive.

My heart always warmed to the simplicity of this idyllic countryside. It had rained earlier in the day and now the corn fields appeared draped in a wraithlike mist which added a degree of romanticism to my already rose-tinted image of farming life. I had always been attracted to farm life, even as a young child. I always imagined the farm of my dreams, wrapped in rain. I always pictured myself beneath a lone tree with a spreading umbrella top made of big, shading leaves. And the tree stood strong in a huge canola field. Yellow flower bursts all around me were answering in waves to the beat of falling water. I could almost feel the droplets of pure nature upon my skin as they nourished both my body and the canola where it grew ready to harvest. The blooms would always play around my legs like a golden ocean. And there would be a cow—far off in a pasture. I could just see her, at the edge of my dream, and watch her nibbling contentedly on the blooms within her reach. Canola flowers, I imagined, were much tastier than the plain old grass in her pasture. Her name was Patches and I loved but spoiled her.

I only imagined one cow and one canola field since I knew I would not want to work too hard on this farm. It was a dream after all; why spoil it with backbreaking reality?

It was this very daydream of my canola farm which, each time I had it, reminded me of my family. Both my father and my mother had roots embedded in my heart. One branch, connecting me with my father, made me yearn for the pastoral life. While the other, perhaps an even deeper root into my core, caused me to be repulsed by the hard work associated with such an existence.

My father always loved the feel of soil in his hands, as I do. My mother always advocated that dirt was dirt and to keep it out of her house! It simply caused her more work! I find that I like to keep the "great outdoors" outside too. Still there is something about that imaginary canola field that calls to me in the swaying of the stalks and glinting of the yellow blooms in the hot sun—after that rainfall.

My drive led me past corn and even canola fields, grain fields, and vegetable rows. I could imagine my father's thoughts as he made this very trip on his journey toward the mighty Niagara, after Elmwood.

* * *

While driving south toward the Niagara Region, which my parents had agreed was a safe and industrious place to relocate to, my father saw a farm for sale. He came from good farming stock in Belgium, or at least he thought he did, from somewhere in his ancestry. So he stopped in the town nearby to talk both of my uncles, who traveled with him, into buying farmland in the area. They disagreed so he called my mother. Five thousand dollars for a hundred-acre farm. And more land would be made available once the farm became successful which, of course, my father saw as inevitable.

I am forced to reveal something about my father here. He was a dreamer to some extent and he did not know how to farm anything. He had no idea how to cultivate land on a large scale or how to rear livestock. But in his dreams, he argued, "How hard could that possibly be?" He was willing to work hard for his imagined, idealistic, pastoral tranquility. My mother was told how she would love working a farm with animals around her and her children growing up free.

My mother once told me what she had answered him at that time. She told me on a day during which *my* dreaming had sent me to her to ask why our farm had never come to be a reality. My father had never stopped talking about it and I had absorbed that dream from him. What a surprise!

She told me that she had witnessed poor farmer's children in Belgium. Not one of them had been bathed regularly or thoroughly ever in their lives—and their parents were old before their time with the never-ending work. She had argued that this vision he had of farming life was a ridiculous fantasy and not something she wanted for her precious sons or for herself. If he bought the farm, he would be living on it alone. She would stay in Elmwood with her boys!

Her answer made me see, immediately, that my father's vision and my canola farm were as one. They were both unrealistic and impractical. She had known this instinctively.

Therefore, the farm plan was out! My father would never have risked his wife's unhappiness in any way. He drove down to Niagara to see what that region of Canada could offer. What he found, back in 1954, was lumber yards and lots of construction going on. The region was prospering through the influx of new immigrants seeking shelter from the devastation of what was left of their homes in Europe. An added plus for my father was that no one and nothing bore a German name. That cinched the deal for him. He and my uncles took a job in one of the lumber yards which had expressed an appreciation for their knowledge of the different types of lumber and their specific purposes in the construction industry. They became skilled labourers who were in high demand in Niagara.

They found a home in a basement apartment. And the upstairs neighbours were cleared by my father as wonderfully friendly Italians who knew how to cook. They fed him when he signed the papers for the apartment and that was always a way to my father's heart. Soon my mother and brothers moved in and life went on. Still my father always thought and talked longingly of the farm he had wanted and never got. I think the notion was rooted in his PTSD; he never stopped wondering about the oblivion which the secluded life on a large farm might have given him. His great love for his family won out. And my father lived with his PTSD in an everyday struggle that no one outside our family witnessed.

One of his sisters and her husband moved to a different area in Southern Ontario. They did get a farm and found that their new god, Jehovah, was a comfort to them. My uncle must have been very attracted to the fact that Jehovah's Witnesses were an organization that rejected allegiance to any country. I believe it was his way of ensuring that neither he, nor his son, would ever fight in any future war.

My father did not see his brother-in-law's faith as anything more than a farce. My uncle's Jehovah was a mere pretence to take his sister away from him. He had spent such a long time convincing his sister to come to Canada after he had fought his way back to his parents' home in Belgium, that the effrontery of her husband earned that man my father's undying hatred. Why was his sister's husband putting her in danger? *Jehovahs were taken first, always, along with the Jews...*

My father never spoke much to them again. Any god was one god too many in his eyes. His sister suffered his absence for her strong connection with their new church. He suffered her presence in his life no more. It was truly a sad set of circumstances. All three men had issues after the war and for my uncle to find peace in his Jehovah was truly a godsend to him. He, at least, had found his tranquility.

My other uncle, who remained close to us for the rest of his long life, also returned to his God here in Canada. He felt it was definitely safe to do so, thousands of kilometers from where his faith had been tested. He saw no threats where my father feared endless challenge. He attended church willingly while my father slept in the pews during

Mass. My uncle never spoke of his faith to me or to anyone in our family. My father never spoke about faith or spirituality of any kind—ever. My uncle's family worshipped and praised while ours suffered doubt and unending issues surrounding our Catholic ties through our school and church. We listened while our father constantly challenged both, verbally and through his actions.

Still, he was a very good man.

Our family's closeness with my God-loving uncle remained a mystery to me during my childhood, until I realized that at no time did a religious or spiritual discussion ever enter into our relationships. Our two families moved into two houses built behind the lumber yard where my father and uncle worked, and we prospered there. I was born and my twin brothers were saved. My uncle thought they were saved by God. My father beat up the man responsible for the threat to his sons.

And I was always left wishing that my father could hear God's intervention.

The difference was that I wanted God, while my father berated Him.

It was as if I heard blue jays and sparrows calling, I heard loons whispering while my father constantly listened to the chaos of life—trucks zooming down the road and men shouting orders or guidance in the lumber yard. But I understand now that his diligence at ignoring his dreams of tranquility in God's world made my relationship with God possible. I could grow up safe, with him to listen for the roar of adversity which assailed him at every turn in his road through life. He protected me. He gave me the choice to love God or to reject Him. He had had no choice in the matter—once his God had died in Halberstadt.

* * *

My father and my uncle had walked back to the lumber yard after lunch with their families. They had been unloading huge slabs of wood from incoming trucks all day. Being a small man, my father had developed an ingenious way to do this without having to take the full weight of the lumber. He and my uncle took turns on the truck pushing the planks to the edge of the flatbed where they rocked the large sheet of wood up to slide it down to the man below. The man below would grasp the edge of the board and the one above would rock the cumbersome sheet toward the stacking skid. The man below simply followed the rocking motion and gave the massive piece of wood a quick shove to transfer the weight to the new location. All it took was a good heave from thigh, arms, and back. It made them feel very alive. They were strong men doing heavy work that required some thought to make it possible. They were thinking men despite the menial labour they performed. They figured it out and they were respected for it. Everyone recognized the survivor's spirit in them both.

My mother was doing the lunch dishes as she watched her boys outside on the driveway. The boys were four and seven years old so they were allowed to play outside alone if she could see them. They were building a fort out of an old box. It was a very big box and the twins loved to get inside to "decorate" the interior of their fort. She saw her oldest boy run off to find some more supplies, she supposed, and the other two climbed back into the box both laughing and giggling. She could hear them through the open window. She stacked the dried dishes and was putting them away when she heard the truck. There was not supposed to be a truck at this end of the lumberyard. The drivers had all been told there were young children playing near the houses at the back of the yard. She went to the window to take a look. Something was not right.

The truck hit the box on the driveway—sending it flying.

My mother screamed.

My father heard the scream. He recognized the sound. It was the sound of love tearing from the soul. It was a sound he had heard many times. But he had never heard it here in Canada. The scream echoed and seemed to go on forever. The retching of his stomach convulsed him and the echo flicked a switch in his soldier's brain. Full survival mode clicked in and he ran. There was no beginning to his run; he did not know that his feet were moving. His steps took him through hell.

He ran through fields of death and rancid smoke. He ran to beat the bombs falling all around him. He ran from the sounds of his friends dying. He ran through screaming and echoes of screaming until he smashed through the kitchen door. He ripped it open and the screaming grew louder. His bile rose as he awakened from his personal horror only to witness the stark emptiness on my mother's blanched face.

She suddenly stopped screaming.

She softly whispered, *"The boys. The box."* Her breath had stopped in her throat and she could say no more. They both ran then. They ran to where the box had landed—upside down on the grass.

My father picked up a corner of the box with hands gentled by fear.

The three boys jumped from behind the corner of the house, dropping the sticks and stones they had been carrying.

My parents' tears would not stop as they ran to the boys. The boys were also crying and screaming now. My mother was holding all three of them.

That is when the blood lust sprang into my father's eyes.

Through clenched teeth, he asked what had happened.

All that my mother could say was, *"A truck."*

My father instantly knew what had happened. He now noticed the truck stopped shortly past the back of the house. The driver was just getting out, probably taking a look behind him at the commotion.

His feet had not yet hit the ground before my father's fist found him. First to the face—surprise him. Then to the body—*kill* him. My father, the soldier, had been well trained. My father, the man, was in a rage of horror, emotionally numbed to what he was doing.

No one threatened his family.

* * *

The boy had been a cigar maker; the man had become a trained assassin.

* * *

My mother, who told me this story, always thought that the driver had survived only because my uncle was there to save my father. He had ripped my father from the driver's limp body and revived them both.

There were no arrests. Both men were innocent. Both men were badly hurt although to look at him, my father had no mark upon him. Both men had done things that they would never do again. And while my uncle prayed, my father cursed and frightened his family.

A new fence was built that day.

My father did not return to work for a week.

And I was born.

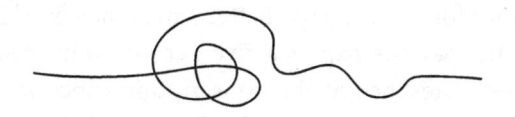

Felt in the Heart

Fence or no, my father refused to live in that place for any longer than it would take to find a new home. He had saved for a down payment, so he would protect his family elsewhere. He quit his job at the lumber yard and began driving a cement truck. His knowledge of the construction industry served him well in that field as well.

But my father's PTSD kept him incomplete—totally without friends. Therefore, my mother did not seek out a bosom friend either. They *alone* were the two cogs on either side of the wheel that was their family. They, alone, made one another whole.

Quietude grew around them. Where they walked together, no one could intrude. Not even their beloved children. PTSD muffled our family in cotton wool. We children were safe and we knew we were loved, yet, as a family, we were separate and isolated. None of us ever knew what would awaken the kraken again. So none of us invited friends to play, there were no sleepovers, but there was always caution as our companion.

I will not be so bold as to say that I personally changed my father. He was still a hardened man who would do anything to protect his family from what he had been through. But having a daughter did make him more pliable. He was never again so fierce; he was, however, very calculating and determined to outsmart any government institution. The perfect example of that was the fact that he never took his sons to Belgium, not even for a short visit. The Belgian government claimed its sons for the army no matter where they lived in the world. I remember the day the papers arrived at our home requesting my oldest brother's presence at the conscription office in Antwerp. It arrived at our home through special delivery mail, in Canada.

My father raged for quite some time and my brothers knew they would never set foot on Belgian soil during his lifetime. He raged and then, years later, he rejoiced when I became of an age when I wanted to join the Canadian army. The rejoicing was due to the fact that my eyesight kept me from being desired by the armed forces. Probably the fact that I could not see the broad side of a barn deferred their choice. And he was happy for the first time in my life that I wore Coke bottle bottom glasses! He figured some good man would learn to love me despite the fact!

* * *

As I said, my being a girl changed my father's choices about how he would unveil any of the fears he still held inside himself. My brothers were expected to man up and understand. I was heavily shielded from any displays of his succumbing to the threats all around him. But there were times when the terrors he envisioned became all too real for him to bury under a veneer of bravado.

It was summer, which meant no school. I was sixteen. I had never experienced any kind of trauma. My father was very good at shielding me. I remained naïve for many years thanks to his ministrations, but I totally appreciated what he had done for me. We were very happy together.

My mother and I loved to sleep in. My brothers were away from home. They already lived elsewhere. My father enjoyed very early morning coffee. Black and cold! He always sat on the couch and watched the news before work. That morning, August 25, 1974, an accident shattered my father's hold on reality. The news channel forgotten, the mason jar slipped from my father's hand and shattered against our small coffee table. I heard the crash as I lay in bed, then my father taking the stairs two, maybe three, at a time. He woke my mother while I ran to my bedroom door. Then as he dragged my mother toward the stairs, he grabbed my arm in a brutal grip. He was dragging us away from some unplumbed danger and our calm world was shattered to bits and pieces. I heard nothing, felt nothing, and questioned nothing. I guess that is what fear does to me. Finally, halfway down the stairs, my mother's voice penetrated my senses.

"*Wat ist, Staf? Wat ist?*"

She was breathless and asking my father what was wrong in Flemish. It was the only clue to her terror that she had forgotten her English. But the sound of her voice brought my senses back online.

As we reached the bottom of the stairs, I saw the broken glass on the living room floor and the drip of coffee over the lip of the table— spreading a deep bloodlike stain across the carpet. I tried to stop but my father was shoving me ahead of him into the basement. Only my mother's scream stopped him from tumbling us all down the steep stairs in his panic.

He stopped and stood still. His eyes reflected nothing. His fear was palpable. I could taste dread in my own mouth and I retched at this new reality. We had no idea what was happening, and I remember my mother's hands upon my father's white face, her voice in the half-light asking what was wrong. She told him that nothing had happened in such a long time . . . why was he so terrified? What had happened?

He was shaking. He was crying. He would not let go of the death grip he had upon me as I teetered at the top of the cellar steps. He told her he had felt the bombs fall. He said, "Bombs are falling around us!"

I heard my mother gasp for breath.

Being young, I had assumed that PTSD had a shelf life and that it had passed through my father's psyche, leaving what was left relatively undamaged.

I was wrong.

My mother, having been schooled by war, knew what to do. She did what she had done in the war years. She headed for the radio. She coaxed my father to come back into the kitchen so that they could verify what had happened through the news station reports. The news told of a bridge collapse. A ship had hit Bridge 12 along the

Welland Canal in Port Robinson, Ontario. The six-hundred tons of the bridge's cement counterweights hit the ground on either side of the canal, just a few kilometers from our home. My father had felt the earth tremble and had heard the tremendous crashes. And in that very instant, his brain had *again* snapped into survival mode.

My father's bombs had fallen; they had fallen in Port Robinson.

The "bombs" had hurt no one.

No one except my father.

Huddled on the couch, my arms still frantically clutched in my father's hands, we cried the tears of PTSD.

That was the day that the only important thing to me became my parents' happiness. I never wanted to see their fear again. I never wanted to be afraid like that again. I wanted to share their suffering with the world so that no one would feel that way—*ever again*. I wanted to write to save myself along with any others who still suffer with PTSD.

Because there have been many wars. And the most horrid things in the world cannot be imagined or even touched, but they can be felt in the heart.

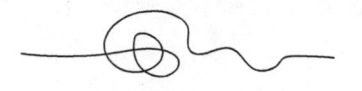

Epilogue

I survived my father's demons. They taught me how to live.

I am my mother's daughter. That inheritance saves me from being too harsh.

I learned from them both that family is the best gift that life can give.

I do wish that, if I reached out my hands, I could touch their faces still. I would return my hands to my own face to check the furrows and lines there which now match theirs—as I remember them.

I realize that this account of madness—of being so undone by anguish that life becomes impossible—is, oddly, about my own life. My life—lived vicariously through my parents' memories and experiences.

Writing it out has let me find my adytum. It is, as Alphonse de Lamartine wrote, a "sweet resting place of the soul, the gloaming wherein my heart finds peace."[4]

Let us all walk where finches gather. Let us hear them chirp joyfully as we walk among yellow blooms. Let us allow our good memories to sprinkle happiness onto our hearts. Let us remember the scents of the home air which made us one unit—*family*.

> This is my father's world.
> And to my listening ears
> It became a difficult place.
> O let me never forget
> That though the wrong often seems so strong
> The battle is not done
> But often won.

---

[4] Quotefancy, Updated: 2024, *Top 120 Alphonse de Lamartine Quotes*, April 19/2024, https://quotefancy.com/alphonse-de-lamartine-quotes, Quote:#31.

Printed in Canada